J.C. CHAUDHRY

The Incredible **Aakash** Story

J.C. CHAUDHRY

The Incredible **Aakash** Story

J.C. CHAUDHRY

Om Books International

First published in 2022 by

Om Books International

Corporate & Editorial Office
A-12, Sector 64, Noida 201 301
Uttar Pradesh, India
Phone: +91 120 477 4100
Email: editorial@ombooks.com
Website: www.ombooksinternational.com

Sales Office
107, Ansari Road, Darya Ganj,
New Delhi 110 002, India
Phone: +91 11 4000 9000
Fax: +91 11 2327 8091
Email: sales@ombooks.com
Website: www.ombooks.com

Text layout: Shiv Shankar Pandey

ISBN: 978-93-91258-79-5

Printed in India

10 9 8 7 6 5 4 3 2 1

Dedicated to:

My grandchildren—Aayaan Chaudhry, Ashvika Chaudhry,
Aerika Chaudhry, and Anyesha Chaudhry

An Open Letter To The Youth Of India

Dear citizens of tomorrow,

As an educationist, science professor, author of academic books and the father of two grounded, yet accomplished professionals, I take pleasure in the fact that many a young mind was moulded by me. I have seen so many successful professionals take flight into the real world on wings of knowledge and feet of humility. They were grounded enough to aim for the sky and soar high. They know that history is not written by the heart and not the brain and that they must make their hearts strong if they want to make history.

To each and every one of them I have only said one thing: academics help you understand your area of expertise but education makes you who you are. As Guru Rabindranath Tagore once said, "The highest education is that which does not merely give us information but makes our life in harmony with all existence."

You are indeed blessed to be born in an era that is brimming with opportunities, a moment in time when knowledge is yours for the asking and your career options and means of earning your livelihood are not restricted to stereotypes. Yes, the Covid-19 pandemic has put a spoke in our spirits momentarily, but it has by no means taken away the larger picture from you or tainted your world that is teeming with opportunities.

Never take them for granted. Or treat them as your privilege. Without comparing my youth full of denial to yours full of hope, I will say that I am glad my grandchildren are born in this era.

All I want to say to you, the future leaders of this globe is, count your blessings and fold your hands and bow your head before the superior power, the benevolent God who gave you a comforting home, caring parents, excellent education and a world full of ideas.

Gratitude must be the first lesson taught to each child. We have to teach ourselves to be grateful for every small and big thing that defines our world. Be grateful even for the fact that we were born as humans with a ticking and curious mind. That, my dear children, is the biggest gift of nature.

From earth we were born and to earth we shall be consigned. Life is what happens to us between these two milestones. And life is what we must live to the fullest.

The other most important lesson in life is to learn how to crack your true potential as an individual to the fullest. You have a reservoir of talent inside you, a volcanic eruption that will come bursting through. All you have to do is to unlock this potential with total honesty and humility. Yes, humility is the most important human virtue you need to cultivate. It helps us all to get up every time we stumble and fall along the way, which is often. Remember a diamond only gets its shine after much strife and struggle. There are many people in the world who keep blaming luck for any type of failure in their lives. Such people can never achieve their goals. Luck favours only those who keep on increasing the chances of its occurrence to them.

Keep reminding yourself that you are but one of the residents of this planet and that you must learn to share it with animals, plants and a number of other species. Mastering the art of remaining centred hence becomes crucial. Be so complete within yourself that you learn the art of coexistence. If you are able to remain centred then there is no entrance exam, no job interview, and no written test on earth that you cannot ace. There is no career you cannot excel in.

To quote Swami Vivekananda: "You have to grow from the inside out. None can teach you, none can make you spiritual. There is no other teacher but your own soul."

I wish each one of you the very best from the bottom of my heart.

J. C. Chaudhry
(**Always A Teacher First**)

Table of Contents

Foreword 1

Acknowledgements 5

1. An End And A Beginning 7
2. Family First 17
3. Goodbye To Hathin 24
4. A Professor Is Born 33
5. In Search Of Stability 41
6. An Entrepreneur Is Born 53
7. Aakash–From Institute To Enterprise 63
8. Taking The Legacy Forward 77
9. The Changemaker 86
10. Ed To Ed Tech 96
11. Forays Into Healthcare 108
12. Science And Spirituality 121
13. The Way Forward 135
14. Creating A Legacy From A Dream 143

Foreword

Most people live one life, but there are a few who live many lives in a single lifetime. J.C. Chaudhry, my father, is one of them. This book is a fascinating account of his journey of grit, perseverance, gratitude and success. He started out in life as a nobody, but what he went on to achieve has immortalised him, transforming him from an unknown being to an unforgettable icon.

To me, he is both a father and a super hero, and a warm-hearted and compassionate soul. He taught me life and management mantras that my books at Harvard did not cover. Donning multiple hats with admirable grace, often more than one at the same time, he has played the roles of a teacher, an administrator, an entrepreneur, a numerologist, a philanthropist, a motivator, a devoted family man and a brilliant investor. His has been an awe-inspiring story of growing from dykes of indigence to heaps of wealth that can dwarf many a one-hit wonder. Nothing could hold him or his ambitions back, even when he was selling biscuits as a young boy at a railway station or when he was traipsing across 40 miles in the chilling Delhi cold at 6 a.m. to coach someone and earn an extra hundred rupees.

He never gave up hope when his early educational ventures crashed before his exhausted eyes. He built his empire not just with the help of riches but also with abundant love and respect, the support of a loving family and friends and immense grace from Maa Vaishno Devi.

He is actually an 'Infinity Man', a survivor who thinks on his feet, sprints into action and persists despite setbacks. He approached every conundrum in his life with exceptional conviction and belief in himself. An army of principles can penetrate the places an army of soldiers cannot. This is the way he has lived his life, full of integrity and unshakeable principles. Despite many ups and many downs, he has stood tall thanks to his ethos and convictions.

He built an empire from scratch and has earned success, money and fame, without actually chasing after them. The secret of his success is his honesty and his commitment to his God: 'his students'. However, to me, his greatest virtue is that he did not let success go to his head. His friends remained the same, his routine never changed, his devotion to spirituality continues to be the cornerstone of his existence.

Even today, what makes him emotional is the mention of his parents and their struggle. What moves him is a pilgrimage to the abode of his Goddess who resides in the mountains of Jammu.

Ready to take on any challenge, he remains interested in learning new skills and expanding his horizons. Being in his presence is a sublime experience for me since there is a complete alignment of thoughts, words and actions in him. This book relates his life story in telling detail and it will inspire young people from different backgrounds to believe in themselves and court success unabashedly like he did and never say never. "I can and I will" has been a constant mantra for him. Every page of this biography ratifies it.

The pages of *J.C. Chaudhry: The Incredible Aakash Story* also highlight the test-prep or coaching-class market which is a pillar of education in India. Yet, it remains an unsung hero in the eyes of the blinkered purist. I give full credit to Chairman Sir for giving it the gravitas and relevance it deserves.

I wish *J.C. Chaudhry: The Incredible Aakash Story* and my father's life inspire us as a family to adhere to his principles of simplicity, spirituality and compassion. Thank you, Papa, for all you have done and all the best for building the next splendid phase of your life!

Aakash Chaudhry
Aakashian

I am delighted to celebrate the life of a man who has risen from the dust and made it to the stars in his lifetime. My father's success story is exceptional and unheard of. It is not only the hard work, dedication and passion of this Iron Man which made it possible. A divine force worked in his favour and helped him scale unimaginable heights in such a short span of time. This divine force is behind him because of his pious nature, staunch belief in God, his willingness to help people in times of crises, his determination to contribute to society and his feeling of indebtedness to the Almighty.

I have no words to describe the difficulties J.C. Chaudhry faced on his arduous journey. He beat all odds and pursued his goals with unshakable commitment. There are many examples of people taking the legacy of a business to newer heights, but there is none where an ordinary school teacher and a grassroots professional believed in himself, worked his way up the ladder by first delivering excellence in the field of education, and then pioneered a great business model of education and elevated coaching to a national platform. He achieved all this not through short cuts but by keeping the interests of students as the top priority.

There are many valuable lessons to learn from him and habits that can be emulated by young people and business leaders.

His success story is definitely worth reading about and getting inspired by!

Dr. Aashish Chaudhry

Acknowledgements

My sincere thanks to Mrs. Kamla Chaudhry, Mr. Jai Dayal Chaudhry, Mrs. Pushpa Devi Arora, the late Dr. A.D. Taneja, Mr. Y.K. Gauba, Mr. Y.P. Purang, and Mr. Pramod Sethi.

1

An End And A Beginning

"All I ever wanted to be was a 'good teacher'. Everything else that happened was life's bonus."—Jagdish Chand Chaudhry

A professor of Biology once invited his class to closely observe how a larva breaks through the sheltered walls of a cocoon. He placed a row of cocoons on a lab table. As three dozen bewildered eyes stared, the larvae began struggling, pushing, trying to burst through the delicate walls of their cocoons. Taking pity on them, one of the students cut open his cocoon with a blade. Out flew the larva, but it dropped dead in a jiffy. The other students however, patiently waited for nature to take its course. And sure enough the cocoons unfurled and tired but buoyant larvae flew out and sped away, alive and kicking. The moral of the story: struggle is inevitable, strife is the only route to survival and the chrysalis for eventual perfection.

This is a story Professor Jagdish Chaudhry never tires of sharing with his students, motivating them to push their boundaries and break the glass ceiling. This is the story of Jagdish's life. One that began in a sleepy village in Haryana and spread out into over two decades of teaching at a government school till the cocoon of comfort was broken and the glorious flight into entrepreneurship was launched.

The founder of India's iconic educational enterprise, Aakash Educational Services Limited (AESL), Jagdish is a self-made millionaire who transformed the unorganised world of coaching into a full-fledged industry. He also turned his modest mom-and-pop shop into a multi-million empire with interests ranging from education to healthcare and film-making, and has churned out nearly one-third of the nation's doctors and engineers.

While the science professor in Jagdish acknowledges the hard work that marked his career graph and the accomplished numerologist that he is gives full marks to his harmonious numbers. He often says, "Everyone works hard. But I was fortunate that my hard work paid me huge dividends." Though most of his time was spent playing Excel sheet Olympics with the balance sheet or in the classroom moulding minds, a part of him was lost in another world mastering numerology, understanding the impact of gems on the fate of humans and perfecting ways to calm a frantically racing mind using the sublime tool of meditation.

How many families that start life with seventeen hundred rupees manage to eventually reach a net worth of five hundred million US dollars? How many teachers who teach Biology at a government school in a tony suburb of New Delhi can create an empire that is hailed as "the largest educational acquisition in the world?"

Helming an enterprise that is worth a whopping seventy eight hundred crore rupees today, Jagdish remembers every harrowing moment of his tough initial struggle. The battle he fought first was to rise above the unforgiving drudgery of poverty by virtue of sheer grit, perseverance and his inborn talent to teach. His trusted Major Generals, his sons, Dr. Aashish Chaudhry and Aakash Chaudhry, joined forces with him to win the battle. Aashish is an orthopedic surgeon whose Delhi-based super specialty health care facility, Aakash Healthcare, is pushing the envelope in ethical practices. His younger son, Aakash, Managing Director and Co-promoter of Aakash Educational Services Limited, has helped Jagdish to play the numbers game successfully, taking India's largest chain of coaching centres to a total of 214 and introducing innovative, game-changing practices in education.

To understand Jagdish's journey fully, it's important to rewind to 1947, three years before he was born. The story begins with the life of the man he unabashedly calls his only hero: his father, Nanak Chand Chaudhry.

1947 heralded a new beginning for the Indian subcontinent. It was also one of the most tumultuous of times in history as people were affected by a volatile mix of emotions. The nation had gained independence from an oppressive colonial ruler, but its heartland stood divided, split into two right through the middle. On one side lay a new nation, Muslim-majority Pakistan, and on the other, Hindustan stood, carved out on its west and east ends.

Terrified people from both sides of a recently forged border were fleeing for their lives. They were submerged in a deluge of violence, induced by communal hatred—the culmination of years of the divide and rule policy practised by the British. Leaving behind their homes, fields and businesses to flee to safety, people moved hastily towards a new home: Hindus on one side and Muslims on the other. A long cavalcade of refugees, on foot, in bullock carts and aboard trains and buses were in motion. Many met their end en-route, attacked by mobs of hate-mongers. Many crossed over safely, though devastated in body and shattered at heart by the time they made it to their destinations.

In the far-flung village of Bukshar, Tehsil Rajanpur, Dera Ghazi Khan, Nanak Chand Chaudhry, a farmhand, was planning his next move along with the many Hindu residents of his village. Dera Ghazi Khan was a narrow strip of land sandwiched between the Indus river on the east and the Sulaiman mountains on the west. It relied largely on farming and animal husbandry for a living. Situated at a distance from the border, any exit from the village would entail taking a train to Atari—a means of transport that was being provided by governments on both sides to ferry their people to relative peace and safety.

Nanak Chand knew that he had to head towards Hindustan. But leaving behind all things familiar was a tough call especially when his actions would hold the lives of his five loved ones to ransom. He had to think of his four little children: his eldest son Prabhu Dayal (11), his little daughters, Draupadi and Pushpa and his youngest son, Jai Dayal, a one year old. His wife, Bhagwani Devi, a frail but feisty woman was by his side, in complete solidarity with his plan to move from the village with the five of them to relative safety.

The village had been the only home Nanak Chand's family had known for generations. Leaving it would feel like uprooting a healthy plant, much like the ones he grew with great care in the fields. Right from the day he was born, miraculously so, to a childless couple, the village had been his field and he its crop.

Nanak Chand's mother had been unable to conceive for many years after marriage. Troubled, his father decided to seek help from the gurus who resided in Hardwar. He travelled there and offered himself selflessly to the service of the Guru (Guru Seva). So great was his dedication that a guru blessed him, placed prasad (holy offering) in his palm lovingly and told him to feed it to his wife. This would ensure that they would be parents to a son.

"They were told that it would be a son and he would have a mole on his right side. And if that were true, the child must be named Nanak after the supreme Guru," says Jagdish. A son was born and yes, the mole was there. So, the man the entire family adores and remembers with tears in their eyes even today was named Nanak Chand. And with him, the Chaudhry family tree with a fabled legacy was born.

Born, bred and wedded in Bukshar, Nanak Chand, like the rest of the Hindu residents of his village, finally decided to leave. As the family pottered around packing whatever they could safely carry, memories of a carefree childhood flashed before his eyes. He remembered how he was left motherless at one and brought up by the elders of his closely-knit village. His kind-hearted neighbour, a Muslim lady who looked after him as her own, had even breast-fed him when he was a baby.

All of it had to be left behind because certain factions of humans would have them believe that Hindus and Muslims were at war with each other, a war fuelled by nothing but politically-driven hate. The futility of it all and the uncertainty were perturbing.

His village, like others in the region, had a mixed population. Hindu homes shared walls with their Muslim neighbours, both families breaking bread together and sharing both joy and grief. The decision to move to India by the Hindu residents was greeted with sadness by some of the Muslim residents who become their protectors, walking with them to the railway station, which was located a few miles away.

Many years later, hearing this story more than once from his elder brother, Jagdish came to the conclusion, "All people are not good, and all people are not bad. It's wrong to colour everyone in the same light." This insight became one of his main management mantras. It helped him to sift grain from chaff, enlist a trustworthy group of colleagues and build a business empire backed by their support. He also ensured that these die-hard loyalists grew along with him.

~

Nanak Chand and his family boarded a train that was filled to capacity, twice over. Scared faces and fast-beating hearts filled every inch of the compartment, the doors and the roof. The Chaudhrys found a few inches to crawl into and a harrowing ride later, reached the refugee camp in Atari. Situated at the heart of the struggle, Atari was a village in the holy district of Amritsar. It was three kilometres away from the newly drawn India-Pakistan border at Wagah, and a mere twenty five kilometres from the Golden Temple and the last Indian station on the rail route connecting Lahore, Pakistan with Delhi. History has it that it was named after one of its most accomplished natives, Sardar Sham Singh Attariwala, a General in Maharaja Ranjit Singh's army.

In December 1947, from Atari, the family made its way to yet another camp in Karnal, Haryana awaiting the Indian government's decision on relocating them. People were being relocated according to the regions they came from. Those who belonged to under-developed districts in Pakistan were asked to settle down in equally backward regions of India. The Chaudhry family was sent to Palwal, a quasi town. Much like their village in Dera Ghazi Khan, Palwal was surrounded by a string of backward villages. The town itself was not the plushest of places. Nanak Chand and his family moved to a refugee camp housed within a Hindu school and from there, the family's long years of struggle to find a firm footing in their new surroundings began.

The family was allotted a tent and left to its own resources. There were five mouths to feed and no source of income. Nanak Chand chopped wood, selling it for a few annas and feeding his family humble meals. The Indian government had a clear-cut compensation policy for the refugees and their families. Farmers were offered land in exchange of the land they had left behind. Businessmen were offered assistance in starting their enterprises all over again. And government jobs were given to those who had worked in the bureaucracy. Since Nanak Chand had owned no land or business, he was simply handed a compensation of seventeen hundred rupees to start his new life. Much of this money was used later to repay a loan he had taken from his brother-in-law to educate his eldest son. After paying his brother-in-law fifteen hundred rupees, Nanak Chand was only left with two hundred rupees.

The period between 1948 and 1950 was tough for the entire nation. Along with the trials of the partition arrived the tribulation of a plague that set the already stretched resources of India and its people a greater test of resilience and perseverance. "People did not know what was better: dying of the plague or of hunger," says Jagdish.

After surviving on the meagre earnings from selling wood for two months, Nanak Chand's family moved to Sevli, a forgotten village in the heart of Haryana with no electricity, amenities and roads. They occupied an abandoned house, a one-room establishment, possibly the once-happy abode of a family that had fled to the other side of the border. After much deliberation, it was decided that Nanak Chand would start a business of his own in partnership with someone he could trust.

"My father decided to open a kirana store (small shop selling groceries and other sundry items), with two family friends, Dithu Ram and Nautan Ram, in the neighbouring village of Hathin. The decision was a ray of hope and gave the family a fresh shot in the arm," remembers Jagdish.

Every morning, Nanak Chand would make his way there, work all day, and come home in the evening with his share of the profits. Unfortunately, the shop was robbed one day and this disrupted the family's plans, forcing Nanak Chand to change track. He took a tonga (horse-drawn carriage) on loan and plied it from Palwal to Hodal, ferrying people to and fro. It was a tough job. At the end of the day, he had to pay the owner of the horse as well as feed the animal. The money he earned was not enough to make ends meet. His family was growing and so were expenses. In 1950, Jagdish was born and in the subsequent years, his little sisters Shakuntala and Sarla came along, taking the family count to nine.

Every member of the family made an effort to contribute to the kitty. "My mother took to toiling outside the home too," says Jagdish. "A brave woman, she did not spend even a single idle moment, working all day, running the household, feeding and rearing us kids and also working long hours in the fields. Her contribution to the family's earnings was immense." She was up at four every morning to knead cotton wool. After this, she would work on a farm, threshing wheat and making bundles. If she made twenty bundles she could take one home. She would then cook for her family and when this was done, she would stitch clothes and weave durries (rugs) to earn money.

The two elder daughters washed utensils, fetched water from the well, and lent a hand in the kitchen. The boys worked as farm hands and also made some money by selling soda bottles at the railway station or dal moth on pattals (dry lentil snack served on pouches made of leaves).

"I worked too, selling biscuits that I bought with the eight annas my mother gave me," says Jagdish proudly. Jagdish's entrepreneurial mind was at work even then. He realised that all that he had to do was ensure that he earned back the eight annas he had received from his mother. Thereafter, he could shamelessly devour every biscuit himself.

Despite having endured a tough life full of obstacles and daunting challenges, the Chaudhry family never let go of their optimism. All that Jagdish remembers of his childhood is 'being happy and content' even if those were unimaginable words considering the difficulties they faced. The grit to go from nonce made Jagdish a humble man. He had no qualms about starting his coaching enterprise from a rented, ramshackle room and with a class of twelve aspiring doctors. His early struggles grounded him, turning him into a hardy entrepreneur who never shied away from menial tasks like cleaning his classrooms and sweeping the floor.

The Chaudhry clan never once lost track of their goal in life—to elevate themselves from the drudgery poverty had inflicted upon them. They were determined to rise up and find their way into middle-class comfort. And the key to this, they knew, was schooling and education. Nanak Chand, not an educated man himself, was determined to ensure a better life for his sons. He worked hard to give them an education that would let them move up the ladder and find white-collar jobs. He also married off his daughters to respectable and well-settled families after they completed their schooling.

"Our father is our real inspiration. Not only was his whole life uprooted at the time of the partition, he also lost his soul mate, his wife in 1959," says Jagdish. The children were very young then and Nanak Chand himself was only 42. He could have married again. "In fact, our maternal uncle tried his best to convince him to get married again so that his second wife could be a mother to his seven children." However, Nanak Chand believed that the new wife would lose interest in her seven step-children once she became a mother. Fearing that this would make their life hell, he made the supreme sacrifice. If he had married a second time, fate may have turned in a different direction for the motherless children.

Living to the ripe old age of ninety six, Nanak Chand led an independent, energetic and incredible life. He continued to work in his shop that was located midway between Sevli and Hathin, living on his own till he was in his late seventies, cooking all his meals, washing his clothes and getting along just fine. He moved only when his youngest son, Jagdish, insisted that he shift to Delhi and live with his family. Jagdish's two elder brothers were posted overseas at that time. Jagdish considered it his good fortune that he could look after his father in his old age and reciprocate his love.

Nanak Chand, living with his son who was now affluent enough to enjoy life's luxuries, did not lose his rooted ways. He loved travelling in local buses even when there was a fleet of cars lined up for him. He would hop on to a Delhi Transport Corporation (DTC) bus and visit friends and family living in various parts of Delhi. The affluence of his sons, though a source of great pride, never made him complacent.

His grandsons loved and adored him. Aakash Chaudhry, his younger grandson, insists that there will never be a man like him. "We are all his legacy. When we were children, my brother and I would go to the village to spend our summer vacations with him. He would pamper us, cook for us, spent a great deal of time with us every day." Aashish, his elder grandson adds, "In a way, he also played the role of a father, while Papa was busy helping Aakash grow. He would accompany both of us to all the entrance exams we gave, stay up at night to ensure we studied. He wanted his family to be well-educated and independent. We also learnt the biggest lesson about self-respect from him."

By his own admission, Jagdish was the weakest of the lot in studies. Prabhu matriculated with a first division and Jai was a Maths genius. But, Jagdish refused to believe in being defined by his limitations. His motto was to push the boundaries with unflagging determination and move the goalposts at every step of the way.

Childhood for Jagdish became a manifestation of his theory that more is less and the sky is the limit. He pushed himself hard and learnt to make even the mundane seem magical. Despite the many hardships, he recalls enjoying a carefree childhood, playing glass marbles at the village square, taking endless dips in the village pond, riding buffaloes or collecting trivial things like Coke bottle caps from the neighbourhood railway station where the three brothers sold biscuits, sodas and snacks to add to the family's meagre earnings.

Right up to Class 6, Jagdish did not own any footwear. Young Jagdish made shoes out of cow dung, which he found at a cow shelter on the way to school. He would rush to the shelter, find fresh dung, step on it and wait for it to dry before coating his tender skin with it. With those stinky boots on, he would reach the village well by the school, fill a pitcher of water and wash his 'shoes' away. And each evening, he would beg his father, (who he called Lalaji), to buy him a pair of chappals. After months of pleading, his father grudgingly bought him a pair. With the slippers on, it felt like he was on cloud nine, cruising the sky in his footwear as if it were a grand aircraft.

Bravado was Jagdish's middle name from childhood and a lack of fear, his signature move. Once, he was pushed into the village pond by a friend who knew he could not swim to save his life. A chorus of voices told him to flap his way to safety. He flapped away and on discovering that he had reached the other shore, he learnt to swim intuitively, and jumped right back in and headed to the opposite bank. "I wanted to make sure that I had learnt how to swim," he says. He repeated this feat all afternoon, even taking on bets to see who could swim across the pond faster!

2

Family First

On 16 September, 1959, tragedy struck the Chaudhry family. Bhagwani Devi passed away leaving her family in deep shock. From the day he was conscious of his surroundings, Jagdish had seen his mother working, day and night. And now she was gone...

"She used to be so busy that she had little time to bond with her children or take time out for herself," he remembers. "As a baby I remember wondering whether she actually loved me. Or was she partial to my elder brothers who brought their earnings to her while I ate all the biscuits and remained at a happy no-profit, no-loss status?"

Two incidents from those days are firmly etched on his mind. One taught him to stay honest come what may. The other made him question his place in the family and cemented his childlike belief that he was not the favoured one at home. Playing glass marbles was a popular game when he was a boy. The rules of the game were simple. You struck a marble and it was yours to keep. He asked his mother for one Paisa to buy his first set of marbles to play the game with his friends. She predictably refused, calling it a wasteful indulgence that the family could not afford. He did not understand the word 'no' and crept out of the house with the money in his pocket. He had removed it from his mother's carefully saved, measly earnings.

Later, when he came back with his pockets full of marbles and was seen showing off to his entire brood, his mother asked him where the money had come from. He lied that he had borrowed it from a friend. Not one to give in easily, his mother asked him to produce that friend before her. Detectivelike probing ensued and the culprit admitted he had depleted her savings by one Paisa. She already knew this of course. When pennies are few, the slightest misses are noticed. She threw herself at him, furious. Her hands were throttling his neck in anger. It took the entire sibling battalion's war cry, "Leave him Mother, he will die," to save him.

"I can never forget her saying that if I were to become a thief when I grew up, she would happily have me die right away, even if it was at her hands," says Jagdish.

~

One day, Jagdish, his eldest brother and his friend went to pluck leaves to serve lentil munchies next to the railway tracks. The boys were also carrying a large pile of Coke caps, collected over the weeks. The idea was to place the caps in a neat row on the tracks in the hope that the train would go hurtling over them and flatten the caps enough to turn them into firkaris (spinning tops).

A guard standing nearby saw them littering the tracks and caught hold of all three of them. He accused them of wanting to derail a train. They were locked up in a dark, dingy room with no ventilation. Scared out of their minds, all three screamed, for help. A few nerve-racking hours later, a passerby did hear their cries. He lobbied for their freedom and the guard let them off grudgingly.

They ran home and told the tale to their mothers. At Jagdish's house, only his brother got a hug from their mother. "What about me?" asked a surprised Jagdish. She shrugged. Jagdish was crestfallen. But in his heart, he was sure that his mother loved him and his siblings equally.

"Every mother loves her child. Some explicitly express it. Others allow their actions to reflect their love," he philosophises. He recalls how his mother nursed him with great care when a painful boil appeared on his leg. She would bandage it each day and sit by his side when he howled in pain. She also stood next to him, holding his hand as the doctor operated it under local anesthesia. That day, he knew she loved him just as much as he had loved her all his life.

"The biggest regret of my life is that I do not have a single picture of my mother," Jagdish sighs. Those were not the days of such indulgences. Struggling to sharpen the hazy mental image he had of her beautiful face, Jagdish searched high and low for a photograph of Bhagwani Devi. The search yielded no results, but he found a handmade rug to fill this void. Visitors to his corporate office are greeted by a framed, vibrant ochre and yellow rug, rustic-looking and evidently made by hand, that rests behind his table. The design is similar to the geometric phulkari motifs, a form of hand embroidery practised in Punjab.

This rug was woven by Bhagwani Devi and her daughters in Sevli as one of the many jobs they undertook to add to the family's earnings. She never sold the piece, instead gifting it to Draupadi, her eldest daughter. Draupadi gifted the durrie to her younger sister Pushpa at her wedding. The rug stayed in Pushpa's house in Agra till it was time for her daughter to get married and she decided to add this priceless heirloom to her trousseau. When Jagdish heard about it, he immediately drove down from his home in South Delhi to Agra, begging his sister to give him the rug instead. He convinced his niece that this creation by his mother had an invaluable place in his heart.

~

In November 1959, the Chaudhry family moved to Hathin on the insistence of their maternal uncle Tola Ram Mukhi. He was very concerned about his sister's family and perturbed about a single father bringing up the children on his own. Besides, the family felt that Jagdish was getting into the wrong company and spending too much time in mindless pursuits. The children and their father moved to a house next to their mamaji's home in Hathin where Jagdish lived for six years. Nanak Chand and Tola Ram brought up the kids together.

Tola Ram made a strong impression on Jagdish. He was very strict with the boys and took a personal interest in their studies. He also ensured they lived a fearless and happy life. "Everyone is born with a certain coding by the almighty and we spend all our life decoding it. My uncle was coded with the karma of helping us motherless children through the toughest phase of our childhood. His role in our lives is pivotal," says Jagdish. As a token of gratitude, Jagdish named the dharamshala in the Maa Vaishno Devi shrine he built at Vrindavan, the Tola Ram Dharamshala.

Hathin was a little more developed than Sevli and closer to the state capital. Jagdish recalls the sheer excitement he felt on seeing symbols of modern life in this quasi town. Electricity being one of them, proper, coal-tarred roads being another. The chance sighting of an aircraft that had strayed into their skies would inspire his entire class to rush outdoors. An act of defiance, which he clearly remembers was met with by a round of caning by this furious teacher!

Though loved and pampered in his new home, Jagdish remembers being reminded often of their penniless state by certain members of his uncle's family. The children, for instance, were not allowed to keep the electric lights on in the night to study. The lady of the house reminded them that the electricity bill was "far beyond their means." Undeterred by this, Jagdish and his brother started studying under the street lamp outside the house. What had to be done had to be done. As he was to later write in his book of quotable quotes, "Poverty is no bar for success."

After his mother's death, his sisters took over the role of nurturers. The loss of their mother was deeply felt by all of them. At the time of her passing, his eldest sister was married and the other three sisters were in school. Pushpa and Shakuntala cooked for the family, cleaned the house and did all the household chores. When Pushpa got married, the eldest sister came back to her maternal home to keep house for her brothers. Both the elder sisters took turns to spend three years each in their father's home, looking after their maternal family. "It's not easy to get a married woman to sacrifice her personal life to help her widowed father and little brothers, at the cost of her own family life," says Jagdish. "Families then were closeknit and people were always there to contribute and help each other out."

The Chaudhry home continues to be a close-knit unit living under one roof today. J.C. Chaudhry's sons, Aashish and Aakash, though busy with work, often bond over a game of cricket. Their father discusses business moves threadbare with them in the home library or at the dining table. "We are all ears when the tiger roars," says Aakash. 'Chairman Sir' (as Aashish likes to call him), speaks his mind, and his sons latch on to his every word. Once a strategy is formed, the path charted and approved, the Generals follow their Chief's command. This is the most important lesson the self-made, family driven enterprise has to offer: they speak in one voice and believe in their leader. Jagdish's business instincts and leadership philosophy are respected and followed by all.

Aakash ensures that every action at the Aakash Institutes is taken with the tiger's blessings. "It makes my task easier," he says. An alumnus of Harvard Business School, with a Bachelors degree in Computer Science and an MBA from ISB, Hyderabad, Aakash got a free hand from his father to corporatise the brand and grow it in a systematic, quality-driven way. Aashish, meanwhile, treats Chairman Sir as his sounding board, bouncing all management decisions of the hospital off him. Interestingly, all three have one trait in common: they race towards their goals like the proverbial blinkered horse, eyes trained on action, not the fruits of their labour.

This quest for perfection comes from their beloved grandfather, the original blinkered horse, who worked twelve hours a day. He was so caught up in work that when people asked which class his chora (son) was in, his stock answer was, "How do I know, ask him!" Nanak Chand, however, was well aware of his children's academic progress and insisted they concentrate on their studies.

Jagdish has first-hand experience in the difficulties of pursuing education from a village. Though 87% of Indian schools are based in villages and 90% of these elementary schools are run by the government, education in his view remains a farce and literacy rates an eyewash. Most children are sent to school for the mid-day meals. A reality that was starkly exposed during the Covid-19 pandemic period when many minors were sent off to work in factories and farms by impoverished parents who were unable to afford two square meals a day for them when schools were shut.

"Education in rural India is also gender imbalanced," Jagdish rues. It is not seen as a must for girls who study till Class 6 after which they are married off by their families. Quality of education is a misnomer as teachers are conspicuous by their absence and even when in class, many are least interested in teaching. According to the Annual Status of Education Report (ASER), more than 50% of the students in Class 5 attending rural schools were not capable of reading a Class 2 textbook and could not solve basic Maths questions.

Things become even more challenging once a child from a village decides to break free and pursue academia, in the hope of becoming a doctor, engineer, IAS officer or chartered accountant. Coaching is unheard of, counselling not even an option. Jagdish mentions the dilemma he faced on completing his matriculation. Nobody around him had the foggiest idea about what they wanted to do in life. "We were totally lost and simply joined a Bachelor of Science (BSc) course because everyone was doing that," he recalls.

Jagdish lived a simple life in Hathin during his student years. Cinema was his only love affair. When real life left him perturbed, he found solace in reel life. A chance encounter with the world of celluloid had him hooked for life. On his eldest sister's wedding day, Jai Dayal asked him to accompany him to watch a movie. There was little they could do to contribute to the ceremony. The two of them sneaked away and watched *Jab Pyaar Kisise Hota Hai* starring Dev Anand. While they were at the cinema, their eldest brother had fallen asleep at a cousin's home and as a result, there was none of the brothers were around to see off their sister at the bidai (farewell ceremony). The next day, all three got a severe thrashing. However, Jagdish felt no regret as he had fallen in love with the magical world of cinema. A love affair that would hold him captive all his life. Cinema became an emotional opioid, a ready learning ground for life lessons, the cornerstone of his very existence.

Every movie taught him something valuable about a new aspect of life. Every hero instilled in him the desire to better his own personality. From Dev Anand he learnt of style, from Dharmender how to treat the body as a temple. Amitabh Bachchan made him a go-getter, an angry young man eager to rise to a position beyond his means. And to love his father, he learnt from the matinee idol, Rajinder Kumar. Later on in life, he openly declared his adulation for one of his heroes when he met superstar Amitabh Bachchan in person on the sets of *Kaun Banega Crorepati*, a television show that his company sponsored three years in a row

All his life, Jagdish has found solace inside a cinema hall, watching movies he likes many times over. *Waqt* taught him how life can be unpredictable and tumultuous. Epic movies like *Mughal-e-Azam* kept him spell bound even when he was watching it for the tenth day in a row. *Amar Akbar Anthony* became his first date out with his newly-wedded bride Kamla.

While real life kept him on his toes with no time for fun, movies became his best friends, his emotional outlet. In his youth, he would often head to the cinema hall to watch movies instead of spending his days at school. Real-life problems kept him preoccupied and he missed out on the chance to make friends and enjoy their company. In the absence of flesh and blood friends, reel people and the movies became his best friends.

For Jagdish, cinema was like a lullaby that a child never tires of hearing. He could watch a movie repeatedly, for days on end. He found more and more ingenuous ways to watch them on his shoestring budget. And interestingly, through the special algorithm of life he had conjured up, he managed to compensate for the hours he spent watching movies by studying extra hard.

3

Goodbye To Hathin

Life in a village is idyllic and fairly predictable. You spend a carefree childhood running around in the open, swimming in the village pond, forging deep friendships and studying at a school that has only basic amenities. Once you grow up, you opt for one of the few available means of earning a livelihood.

However, if you have no interest in being a farmer, shopkeeper, or school teacher it is imperative that you make your way to the city. Nanak Chand, firmly entrenched in his own role as a shopkeeper, was determined to make sure his sons moved ahead in life. His eldest son already had a government job after completing college with good grades. The middle son, a genius at Maths, was pursuing a BSc degree in Palwal, opting for the combination of Physics, Chemistry and Maths (PCM). And now it was time for his youngest son to join his siblings in the city.

In 1966, Jagdish completed his matriculation in Hathin. Before joining college he wanted to consult a doctor in Delhi about his left ear, in which he felt he was short of hearing. Nanak Chand handed Jagdish an allowance of Rs. 10 and packed him off to his big brother's house. This sum included the ticket fare, plus a princely daily expense account of one rupee. Jagdish was thrilled at the thought of travelling alone in the train, going to Delhi and being with Prabhu Dayal whom he admired a great deal. This would be his first taste of the big city.

Excited at the prospect, he boarded the train to Okhla Railway Station. A cousin who lived in Zamroodpur (Kailash Colony) had volunteered to pick him up when he landed in Delhi. He settled down in a reserved compartment, the ten rupees parked in his pocket and a happy smile plastered on his face. Suddenly, a slick-looking vendor with a shrill voice caught his attention. The man was trying to sell a watch, perfume, a comb, talcum powder and other such products. The sparkling watch caught Jagdish's fancy. He had never worn or possessed one before.

He was very excited when a co-passenger bid for it at one rupee. Someone else instantly raised the bid to Rs. 3, then 4, and finally 7. Competing with the bidder from the other end of the compartment, Jagdish took it to a whopping Rs. 8. The watch was his and the vendor happily handed over his bag of products to the delighted young boy. Someone joked that he must be getting married to need all these toiletries and objects of desire. Jagdish was oblivious to the jibes, thrilled that he had bought the watch for a steal even if that left him with only two rupees to spend in Delhi.

On reaching his cousin's home, he impatiently tore open the packet and wore the watch on his wrist. Half an hour later, he realised that the hands were stuck and the dial, static. Despairing, he turned to a friend who took him to a watch repair shop. The technician opened up the watch, and lo and behold, inside its body resided a magnet and a few strips of paper! It was a mere toy. The perfume he had bought on inspection turned out to be scented Mobil oil and the talcum powder, flour. Jagdish had had his first brush with orchestrated fraud by gangs known to fool hapless train travellers.

Too ashamed to tell his brother about his mistake, Jagdish quietly accepted the two rupees his brother had given him just before he left for work. Now he had only four rupees with him. He spent this on 'gourmet fruits,' which he had never seen before. First, he bought thirty two bananas for two rupees (a bargain, he felt), which he ate at one go, battling a stomach ache thereafter. And then there was discovery number two in the heart of Lajpat Nagar market. He found a hawker's cart laden with a delicious-looking sugarcane snack. The nuggets were peeled and placed on a bed of ice. This snack, gandheri, sold in the busy bazaars of Delhi, was new to him. He had eaten sugarcane in the fields and devoured its juice, but never eaten it in this neatly shelled and frozen form. He spent two rupees on the gandheris and relished every bite.

The next day, his brother took him to All India Institute of Medical Sciences (AIIMS) to consult an ENT. Back in his village, he was used to taking off his shoes off at the door when he visited the doctor. At AIIMS, he did the same. Embarrassed, his brother told the doctor not to mind his brother's ways since he was a villager who was not used to the city. "I understood what he said and it hurt me," says Jagdish. "But in hindsight, he was right. I was naive. So naive that I mistook the abbreviation 'DTU' plastered on all the buses for the name of a friend in Hathin who had prominent buckteeth and was lovingly called Datu by all of us. I remember asking my brother why Datu's name was inscribed on every bus. Little did I know that it was the short form of Delhi Transport Undertaking."

~

In 1966, when Jagdish bid goodbye to Hathin and moved to Palwal to complete his pre-university and pre-medical at G.G.D.S.D. College, he was very excited about living in a city with a cinema hall. His brother wanted him to take up Maths, but Jagdish suspected that if he agreed, he would become an 'academic slave' and have a sword held to his head at all times by a brother who was obsessed with the subject. In order to protect his freedom, he opted for PCB (Physics, Chemistry and Biology).

Life in Palwal was uneventful. Jagdish still wore a striped pajama to college, a garment men in North-Indian villages typically wear. There were no trousers in his humble wardrobe even though he had gone hoarse asking his eldest brother for one. In Palwal, all he had was his middle brother to keep him on a tight leash and a boring half-baked town to wander around. The only respite was that there was a picture hall in town and he no longer had to catch a bus like he used to in Hathin to watch a movie. He binge watched movies in his inimitable style. Every week, he would save up six annas to afford two tickets at three annas each and end up seeing the same movie twice.

Most of the students in Jagdish's class hailed from nearby villages and none of them had the courage to question the professors when they were confused about academic questions. Jagdish remembers his encounters with Dr. Aggarwal who taught him Botany. In the lab, when students were asked to dissect a stem-section, mandatorily cutting it in a straight line, the angry professor would rush towards Jagdish's table, pick up the stem and chuck it in the wash basin screaming "leak." Jagdish could not understand what he had done wrong or what was leaking. Nor could he muster the nerve to ask. It was only many years later when he himself, as a professor of Botany, corrected a student who was cutting a stem in a slanted way by saying "oblique," that he understood what Dr. Aggarwal had been trying to tell him.

A life-changing event happened in the Chemistry lab during Jagdish's student days at Palwal. His professor was teaching the attributes of pure chlorine, especially its pungent smell. The students were asked to inhale a whiff of it. Over-enthusiastic Jagdish inhaled a large amount, coughing, sneezing and choking on it for a full hour thereafter. The trauma scarred him for life as he lost his sense of smell after this. Good, bad or ugly, fragrant or foul, his nose was deprived of all smells forever.

This loss became both boon and bane in his life. Once, when he could barely smell his female colleague's generous dose of perfume at BITS Pilani (where he did his post graduation), he was 'thrashed' by her for not giving her a compliment. On another occasion, when he was faced with the prospect of sweeping the floor of his new institute in Ganesh Nagar along with the administrative in-charge, his nose came to the rescue. The students complained of a foul smell and the administrative in-charge too was troubled by it. But Jagdish swept the floor happily in the absence of the house-keeping lady since he was immune to the smell.

~

After completing his pre-medical, Jagdish moved to Jalandhar to join DAV College at the start of 1968. Jalandhar was a university town, much bigger and livelier than sleepy Palwal. When he made the move, he requested his middle brother to go with him and make sure he settled down there. Jai was living in Kurukshetra at the time and Jagdish asked him to come down to his city from where the two would set off to Jalandhar. Before that, they would visit Amritsar and see the Golden Temple, something they had always dreamt of doing.

The two took the train to Amritsar where they planned to spend half a day. However, their journey from Kurukshetra to Amritsar turned out to be quite a thriller. Since he clearly remembered how he had been duped on the train to Delhi when visiting his elder brother, Jagdish decided to retire safely to the upper birth. Meanwhile, a burly Sikh who was magically turning a limp cord into a serpentine coil cast a spell on his brother who was sitting a few seats ahead. The Sikh challenged some of the co-passengers to run a pencil through it, promising them a one-rupee reward if they succeeded. Many tried the trick and magically aced it. Chaudhry senior too wanted to try his hand at it. He fell into the trap and lost five precious rupees in the bargain.

Catching the drift instantly, Jagdish tried to rush to his brother's side to stop him but was blocked from doing so by two muscular men. Later, after the men jumped off the train, a lady sitting next to them told them that they were lucky that they lost. Had they won, the goons would have beaten them up or thrown them off the train to retrieve their money.

The brothers got off at Amritsar station, shaken and scared, still smarting from the nightmare. As they made their way out, they were ambushed by men calling themselves sevadaars (volunteers) who offered to help them, take them to the temple, and find them a cheap hotel. They were further petrified and chose to go to a dharamshala instead, shelving the idea of visiting the Golden Temple completely. The train to Jalandhar was in the wee hours of the morning and they decided to catch a bit of sleep. But they were too scared and restless to fall asleep and ended up taking refuge at their eternal 'happy place,' the movies. *Humraaz*, a suspense thriller starring Sunil Dutt and Raj Kumar, was playing and they bought tickets for the late-night show.

Once again, cinema had come to Jagdish's rescue. As for Amritsar, "The fear of the city remained deep in my psyche. Even till the mid nineties when it was time to open an institute there, and I had to take a trip to the city I feared most," he says. He did go on to realise how unfounded this fear was when he spent time there and befriended many endearing people in the city.

~

Jagdish has always believed that a guru plays the role of God in a student's life. He often compared a student to wet clay, easily moulded by a competent teacher. He formed this opinion after closely observing teachers he met, first as a student and then as a professor. As a student, he was unimpressed by most of them, feeling that he would benefit more, were he to study the subject on his own. This helped him to define the role of a teacher clearly for himself and the thousands he was to employ at his institute.

During his one-year stint at Jalandhar, Jagdish was fortunate enough to meet a guru who became his muse for life. This was a professor of Botany named Mr. Widge. Professor Widge made the subject so interesting that young Jagdish hung on to every word he said in class. It was his teaching style that made Jagdish fall in love with the subject and inspired him to become a teacher. This story did not have a rosy start though.

Professor Widge was enraged when Jagdish unwittingly broke the lens of a microscope in class. "Did you not learn something as basic as handling a microscope?" he yelled. His student's honest answer that he was never taught to, melted Professor Widge's heart. He went on to sit next to Jagdish and teach him everything about handling the instrument.

From that day on, Jagdish became his favourite student. Widge Sir followed the practice of selecting toppers through class tests and creating a pool of promising students. Jagdish was the first one to be selected in this pool. This changed his own perspective of academics forever. He was filled with confidence and felt a burning desire to excel. He was seen making a beeline for the library where he would sit for hours, reading, memorising and frenetically filling up reams of paper with his notes. He was so well prepared he could complete his test papers in record time.

Successful people have a few trademark traits. For one, they are obsessive about things that catch their fancy, tug at their heart or pierce their soul. Jagdish was a blinkered horse too, chasing things that interested him with a junoon, a streak of madness. If he wanted to master something, he wouldn't rest till he did. Simply because he could not read the Urdu poster of a film starring his eternal hero, Dev Anand, he learnt to read the complex language in four days flat!

Jalandhar was the first upwardly-mobile phase in Jagdish's life. For one, he became the proud owner of a pair of trousers that he wore to college every day. His big brother had finally given in and donated one of his old trousers to Jagdish and Bhagwan Tailors had altered the pair to fit him. A trouser is not just a trouser, especially if it is the only one you posses. All through the week, it was worn with great pride and then every Sunday, washed and left to dry in the middle of the hostel room that he shared with a fellow student called Jindal. When Jindal complained about the stink of the trousers and flung it across the room, Jagdish was furious. He slapped him across his face. He told him that if he could not stand the smell, he could leave the room till the trousers dried.

~

In 1970, Jagdish graduated in Science, completing his third year of graduation from Government College, Gurgaon. A small-town lad who rarely ever spoke to girls and had safely remained in an-all boys' ghetto, he was overwhelmed when he entered the college. At that time, it had a student ratio of 80% girls to 20% boys. He recalls staring in bewilderment at the campus buzzing with girls, where boys were a rarity. He was gawking away out of curiousity but the stare cost him dearly. The Principal, Jaswant Kaur apprehended him and asked him about his antecedents. She ordered him to get a character certificate from Jalandhar before joining the college.

Gurgaon at that time was not the mini New York like the sleek Gurugram of today. No sky-scrapers dotted the horizon and nor were there any office complexes in the locality. It was just one of the three 'village towns' that surrounded the grand capital city of New Delhi. Jagdish rented a one-room tenement next to the Bhuteshwari Temple in Gurgaon. Some of his friends rented tenements next door. Recreation for these boys was about eating out, chatting and often striking a bargain to buy the entire merchandise off some of the hawkers they ran into on the streets.

Jagdish discovered yet another way of watching movies without investing in tickets here. The movie playing in the hall next door was *Phool Aur Pathar*, which was four hours long. When Jagdish went to see it for the first time, he noticed that there was no watchman at the gate and by interval time the gate was left unattended. For the whole of the next week, he saw the movie post the interval for free!

~

Jagdish was one of many students who had completed his BSc course and was clueless about what career to pursue. He only knew that he had to add a Masters tag to his CV. While a student emerging from a public school in a metropolitan city is swamped with choices, in the smaller towns of India, Medicine and Engineering remain the first choice.

Going on to teach in a college in a backward town and in government schools from 1974 to 1993, Jagdish closely observed the struggle of students from humble backgrounds who aspire to join professional courses but are short on information about how to go about it. They lacked access to coaches and counsellors. So, when he established Aakash Institute, he went on to launch a unique programme under which fifty seats are reserved for students from economically weaker sections every year. Twenty five seats are for aspirants to the medical stream and twenty five to engineering. Students have to pay only the registration fees and the management writes off the rest of the fees. Selection to this course is via an entrance exam and the most important criterion is that applicants should have studied in a government school since Class 8 and must appear for their final Board exam also from there.

The stark contrast between urban and rural students, which Jagdish was well aware of, dawned on his son Aakash while counselling students in a leading Mumbai school. On asking how many children wanted to pursue medicine, Aakash saw only a handful of hands go up. The class wanted to pursue career paths that were as varied as a chef to an astronaut.

Keeping the urban-rural gap in mind, Aakash Educational Services Ltd consciously expanded in a democratic manner across the country when it took off. The management laid special emphasis on counselling at the grass-root level, making students aware of the myriad job opportunities open to urban students. Aakash helped students take a well-informed decision. They penetrated deep into the country taking their Joint Entrance Examination (JEE) and National Eligibility Entrance Test (NEET) programmes to places as far flung as Jorhat in Assam and Jabalpur in Madhya Pradesh. Jagdish proudly declares today, "Name a city and we are there!"

4

A Professor Is Born

Jagdish has always believed that success is a solitary journey undertaken by those who have the determination to reach their goals despite all the obstacles that line their way. A mindful pursuit of perfection is the true hallmark of a leader. Over the years, whether it was his heart ruling his head or his head dictating terms to his heart, he made sure that he ended up achieving exactly what he had aspired for.

After his graduation, Jagdish drifted into a job Lalaji (his father) got him through a family contact. He joined Thomson Press as a worker. Founded in 1867 by Lord Thomson in partnership with Vidya Vilas Purie, a member of a prominent family of publishers from Lahore, Thomson Press used to print children's books at that time. Today, it is better known as the press that prints the popular news magazine, *India Today*.

Jagdish hated the job and quit within a month. His heart was set on finishing his Masters course. He was selected for the interview at Birla Institute of Technology and Science (BITS) Pilani. Overjoyed by this news, he confidently approached Lalaji and asked him to give him fifteen rupees to travel to Pilani for the interview. His father refused to give him the money and ordered him to abandon all dreams of further studies, which the family could ill afford.

What followed was like a scene out of an Amitabh Bachchan thriller. This angry young man decided to take matters into his own hands.

With four rupees in his pocket, he ran away from home and went to his cousin's house to borrow some money. When he overheard his cousin sharing his whereabouts with Lalaji on the phone, he fled from the house. Hopping on to a three-wheeler, he headed to the railway station. With no money in hand to pay for his ride, he jumped off the racing vehicle as it neared the station and rushed in, blending into the crowd. His interview was scheduled for 11 am the next morning and he had only nineteen hours to get there.

After a long wait, he managed to catch the midnight train to Jaipur and got off at Loharu at dawn. From there, he had to catch a bus to Pilani but, much to his chagrin, the ticket was far beyond his means. Undeterred, he decided to race to Pilani, which was 24 kilometres away! He reached the university campus at 10 a.m., covered in dust and totally dishevelled.

Arjun Dev Taneja, professor of Physics at BITS and a close associate of the Chaudhry family was waiting for him there. Shocked to see what 'the cat had dragged in', Taneja took the bedraggled Jagdish to his house to freshen up. Despite the tough journey to Pilani, Jagdish aced the interview. He was selected to study at one of India's most revered campuses and to pursue a Masters in Botany. There was only one hitch: the total expenditure at BITS would come up to Rs. 150 and Jagdish had nothing with him except his iron will and sharp mind. Both these attributes helped him excel during his student years and as a teacher later on.

At BITS Pilani, he found a mentor for life—Professor Taneja. Thanks to Taneja, he could enroll in a scholarship programme for economically weaker students. The kindly Professor also gave Jagdish a personal loan of Rs. 50 per month. After hearing that his son had been selected to study at BITS, Lalaji's heart melted and he too offered to support Jagdish.

BITS Pilani is a deemed university that offers both under graduate and Masters programmes in pure sciences, technology and Engineering. This was Jagdish's first exposure to a reputed institution that offered quality education. He was quick to realise the difference between BITS and his earlier colleges in terms of quality of education. He also became acutely aware of the significance of teachers who take their role as mentors seriously. At BITS, Jagdish's personal hypothesis on teaching gained a new dimension. He was convinced that a contented teacher teaches well and a nurturing atmosphere motivates a student to learn. These two pre-conditions to create model learning programmes became the foundation of the coaching programmes he would go on to found later on.

Interestingly, it was at BITS that Jagdish spoke on stage for the first time. A much revered speaker whose motivational lectures today attracts thousands of listeners, he recalls being gripped with incontrollable fear, his legs shaking and his palms sweating when he was asked to introduce himself at the orientation programme at BITS. But he managed to conquer his fears slowly and steadily over time.

Jagdish did exceedingly well in his course. When he scored 79% in his Masters, his joy knew no bounds. He realised that nothing interested him more than education. He was convinced that he wanted to be Professor Chaudhry who would mean to his students what Professor Widge had meant to him when he was under his tutelage.

Most colleges Jagdish applied to for a teaching job after completing his Masters were located in the small towns of Haryana. At his first interview at Ahir College, Rewari, the subject expert of the department turned out to be less qualified than him. In the next one at Vaish College, Rohtak, an elderly board member called him a ghas phoos ka doctor (Botany professor) and then threw a real googly at him. He asked him why a big jamun tree yielded such small fruits and why a slender creeper was covered in gigantic water melons. The answer Jagdish gave could easily be listed in the book of absurdities, but it got him the job! He said that if watermelons grew on trees, imagine how dangerous they would be were they to fall on someone's head and cause a serious head injury.

The twenty two-year-old professor was hired at a salary of Rs. 446 per month, out of which Rs. 200 was sent home, Rs. 50 repaid to Professor Taneja, Rs. 34 paid as rent and another Rs. 150 spent at the restaurant where he ate all his meals. The rest was spent on movies. The tradition of watching every movie first day, first show, was kept up and Professor Chaudhry also became the college's unofficial movie critic.

Day one at work turned out to be quite eventful. On the way to class, a student much taller than him tapped him on his shoulder and, in a typical Haryanvi dialect asked, "Naya se?" (are you a new student?). He replied, "Haan, naya se." (yes, I am new). Jagdish was only one or two years older than most of his students. Later, when they settled down in class, Seva Ram, the student, realised that Jagdish was actually the new professor. An embarrassed Seva Ram blushed beetroot red.

Jagdish was assigned the subject of bryophytes. Brimming with confidence, he started teaching the class of second year BSc students about this plant. Half way through the lecture, a student, Archana Aggarwal, asked him three extremely difficult questions. He fumbled and concocted an answer which he knew was wrong. Soon after class ended, he ran to the library and picked up every book on bryophytes. He would read them at home and also make sure that they were not lying around for students like Archana to borrow and realise that he had got the answers wrong.

He read voraciously and studied the subject non-stop for twelve hours, preparing for the next lecture. Here too, he faced a volley of questions from Archana. Except this time, his answers were correct. Every day, he would study for at least 10 hours before stepping into class and every day, Archana would bombard him with questions. She was one of his brightest students who eventually joined an MBBS course. Today, she lives and practises medicine in Russia.

Jagdish is grateful to his students for helping him master the subject and to become a teacher capable of holding his class spellbound. Archana inspired him to study the subject in greater detail and helped him evolve into a better teacher. This made him realise that a good student makes a good teacher and not vice versa.

During his stint at Bhiwani, Jagdish learnt many valuable lessons from his students. He also realised two fundamental truths about himself: he was no sycophant, and he hated cheating and cheaters. Sent to invigilate an exam at Government College, Sirsa, Jagdish turned the

Jagdish Chand Chaudhry, founder of Aakash Educational Services Limited (AESL), is a self-made millionaire who turned his modest mom-and-pop enterprise into a multi-million empire with interests ranging from education to healthcare. (Roy Henderson)

J.C. Chaudhry and his sons, Aashish (left) and Aakash (right), speak in one voice. Once their father charts a path and approves it, the two follow his commands. (Roy Henderson)

J.C. Chaudhry spent his boyhood in a forgotten village in the heart of Haryana. His father ran a small grocery store and the family lived in a small, one-room house in Sevli. Every member of the family including his mother and sisters worked hard to contribute to the family kitty. ©J.C. Chaudhry

In 1966, J.C. Chaudhry completed his matriculation in Hathin and moved to Palwal to complete his pre-university and pre-medical at G.G.D.S.D. College. He was very excited about living in a bigger city with a cinema hall. ©J.C. Chaudhry

The primary school in Hathin where J.C. Chaudhry studied up to Class 5.
©J.C. Chaudhry

A photograph from graduation days. ©*J.C. Chaudhry*

A studio photograph of J.C. Chaudhry after he passed his M.Sc exams. ©*J.C. Chaudhry*

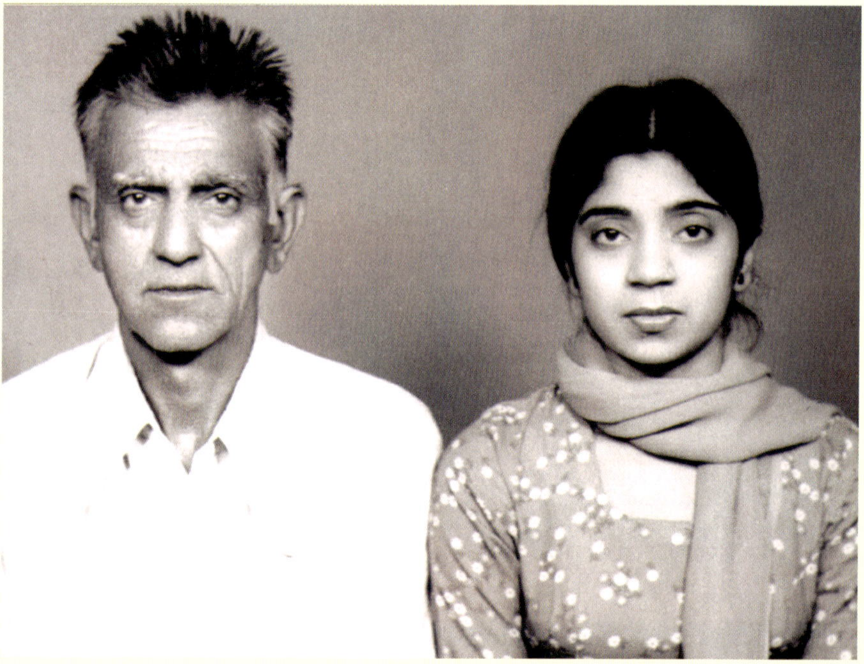

Nanak Chand (seen here with his daughter Sarla Saluja) chopped wood and drove a horse-drawn carriage to fend for his family when he moved to India. ©*J.C. Chaudhry*

J.C. Chaudhry two months before his marriage (in 1977). ©J.C. Chaudhry

An exhausted but exhilarated J.C. Chaudhry when he qualified for the Haryana Civil Services (HCS) in 1976 after preparing for the test for 40 continuous days. ©J.C. Chaudhry

Jagdish and Kamla Chaudhry's saga of togetherness began in 1977. ©J.C. Chaudhry

Despite his father Nanak Chand's reservations, J.C. Chaudhry was determined to keep his wedding a simple, cost-effective and quick afffair.
©J.C. Chaudhry

Both J.C. Chaudhry and Kamla were happy to avoid elaborate tents, lighting, floral arrangements and other paraphernalia at their wedding ceremony. ©J.C. Chaudhry

J.C Chaudhry and Kamla (seen here at the cake-cutting ceremony) entered a new life together that would turn out to be a great roller coaster ride for both. ©J.C. Chaudhry

The first time J.C. Chaudhry and Kamla met, he struck her as an intelligent man with whom she would be able to build a good life. ©J.C. Chaudhry

J.C.Chaudhry riding his Vijay Super scooter with sons Aashish and Aakash. ©J.C. Chaudhry

J.C. Chaudhry with Aashish and Aakash when they had just started their schooling. ©J.C. Chaudhry

J.C. Chaudhry with Kamla and their sons at Katra, where the family had gone for Maa Vaishno Devi darshan in 1985. ©J.C. Chaudhry

Nanak Chand wanted his family to be independent and well-educated. He taught his son and grandsons the value of self-respect. His grandsons loved and adored him. Aakash Chaudhry, his younger grandson, insists that there will never be a man like Nanak Chand. ©J.C. Chaudhry

In 2010, Dr. Karan Singh, Managing Trustee of the shrine at Katra inaugurated the Maa Vaishno Devi Dham, Vrindavan that J.C. Chaudhry built. ©J.C. Chaudhry

The Maa Vaishno Devi Dham at Vrindavan is J.C. Chaudhry's tribute and token of gratitude to the Goddess who has blessed him in more ways than one. ©*J.C. Chaudhry*

A series of ceremonies marked the inauguration of the Dham in 2010, some intimate and only involving the trustees and some having an attendance of over 6,000 devotees. ©*J.C. Chaudhry*

The Chaudhrys, a devout family, are immensely grateful to Maa Vaishno Devi for blessing them with health, wealth and happiness. ©J.C. Chaudhry

Both J.C. Chaudhry and Kamla Chaudhry anchor their lives on Lord Krishna and the symbol of 'shakti', Maa Durga. ©J.C. Chaudhry

At the Maa Vaishno Devi Dham, Vrindavan, besides the pristine temple, the sprawling gardens and the magnificent statue that won J.C. Chaudhry's Jay Kay Trust a place in the Limca Book of Records, *there is also a full-fledged guest house for spiritual residency, a prayer house that can accommodate over 3,000 people, a few acres allotted to an organic farm and another acre for the cow shelter or* gaushala.
©J.C. Chaudhry

The architecture of the Maa Vaishno Devi Dham, Vrindavan replicates the experience of walking to the original shrine at Katra to get a glimpse of the Goddess. ©J.C. Chaudhry

Kamla Chaudhry has had the grit and patience to stand by J.C. Chaudhry's side through many ups and downs. A qualified teacher who opted to play the role of mother, guide and nurturer to her sons, she has always been her husband's pillar of strength. (Roy Henderson)

tables on the students who were used to openly cheating in their exams. He stood on guard, hawklike, during the exam.

After he was done supervising two exams, he was apprehended on the road by a gang of bike-riding students. Exasperated, they demanded he leave Sirsa immediately. They even offered to pay him his fees for the remaining three exams. Though shaken, Jagdish decided to stick around and be the invigilator for all five exams as he had initially planned.

His reputation as a teacher spread far and wide and many students flocked to his modest one-room house in Bhiwani to understand the subject better. Kiran Choudhry, the daughter-in-law of the then Haryana Chief Minister, Bansi Lal, and wife of Chaudhry Surender Singh, was studying pre-medical at Vaish College, Bhiwani. Surender was the General Secretary of the District Congress Committee, Bhiwani. Kiran Choudhry expressed an interest in learning one-on-one from Professor Chaudhry. Surender visited Jagdish at the college and asked him to report to his house to teach Kiran. Jagdish told Surender he was welcome to send his wife for the group lectures he gave at his home every morning at five. Jagdish didn't make house calls and had to pay for it by losing his job.

Even though Jagdish only taught for a year in Bhiwani, he was able to leave a deep impact on his students. Many of them still keep in touch with their former teacher. "Gratitude comes easier to those with limited means," Jagdish points out. "I found greater respect amongst students who were keen to learn but came from humble homes. Also, they had a fire in their bellies to rise above their situation."

~

In 1973, Jagdish went back to Delhi, the city of his dreams, and took up a teaching job at Hans Raj Model School, Punjabi Bagh. It was a Dayanand Anglo-Vedic (DAV) school and he recalls being asked to recite the Gayatri Mantra during the interview. His stint there lasted about a year. He threw himself into the job, striving to fulfill the role of dedicated teacher and supportive mentor. He felt that he was "coded by the almighty to be wedded to a life of karma."

Jagdish mastered the art of keeping his students engaged using innovative teaching strategies. The dedicated Botany teacher also became the resident horticulturist on campus after he constructed a pond in the garden as part of a practical ecology project.

He taught Botany and Zoology to Classes 10, 11 and 12. The school was still building its reputation at that time and the Principal, Mr. T.R. Gupta, asked Jagdish if he was confident to coach his students for an entrance exam. No student from the school had got admission to any MBBS course so far. Chaudhry Sir was given a free hand to coach them and skin them alive if they shirked their studies. Jagdish was confident he would get the required results without resorting to any harsh punishments. He focused his attention on a bunch of hand-picked, nine meritorious students. Under his guidance, three of them, Anjani Charan, Sudhir Yadav and Ashwani Khanna, went on to gain admission at colleges as prestigious as AIIMS and Maulana Azad Medical College.

He met yet another genius who challenged his teaching skills a year later during his stint at Hans Raj Public School. Anjani Charya, who always scored at least 95% marks effortlessly, made Jagdish chew on textbooks twenty times over. Jagdish had to be prepared for any question his student would throw at him. He recalls how Anjani got him to revisit a test paper he had marked, eventually proving that the one mark he had reduced was a mistake. Anjani went home with a score of fifty on fifty and deservedly so.

The stint at Hans Raj was Jagdish's first experience of living in Delhi. Though he was short of money as always, Jagdish lived it up. Every afternoon, he would join a group of friends and head to Standard Coffee House at Connaught Place to sip a cuppa like 'sahebs'. After this, he would catch the bus back to his tiny home in Sriniwaspuri. One day, racked by thirst and with only twenty paisa left in his pocket, he bought three glasses of chilled water and then walked eleven kilometres to get home. What had to be done, had to be done. The heart was meant to rule the logical head...

A year later, the Principal extended Jagdish's probation period at Hans Raj, informing him that he was not ready to be confirmed in his job. When quizzed why, the Principal told him that being honest was not enough, one had to appear honest. Simply put, Jagdish needed to be seen in the staff room after school hours like the other teachers, poring over homework copies of student and checking their papers—not making a beeline for Connaught Place. This was the straight-forward Jagdish's second lesson in diplomacy and dealing with the powers that be, also learnt the hard way!

Jagdish got his first taste of the drill of appearing for an entrance exam when he decided to apply for the Haryana Civil Services. His brother, Prabhu Dayal, who was working in the Ministry of External Affairs, was fully aware of the powers vested in the Indian bureaucracy. He wanted Jagdish to try his hand at the Indian Administrative Service (IAS) and so, he paid the fee of forty eight rupees and enrolled Jagdish for the exam in 1974.

Little did he know that his brother was least interested in a tryst with power. Jagdish went to the Union Public Service Commission (UPSC) office, found out the refund policy and retrieved thirty six rupees, which he splurged on watching movies. He confessed his crime to his brother and in his defense, said that one should only pitch apples against apples. A country bumpkin like him stood no chance at the interview, competing with students who had passed through the exalted portals of Delhi University's St. Stephen's College and Doon School.

His heart, however, was filled with shame and remorse for having let his well-meaning brother down. Later on, when he heard of the Haryana Civil Services exam that would be conducted in forty days time, he told S.K. Arya, a friend who was preparing for the exam that not only did he want to appear for the exam but also make the cut.

Those forty days were a test of his will power. Jagdish and Arya got together and studied round the clock. The dhaba (small eatery) next door was asked to slip a ready-to-eat thali (platter) of three rotis (bread) and a bowl of dal (lentils) under their door twice a day. Eight subjects had to be mastered in forty days, 960 hours and 57,600 minutes. Jagdish managed to score 72% in the exam and make the cut.

However, he knew he could not get any further as the financial means of securing a seat in the Haryana bureaucracy was far beyond his four hundred and forty six rupees monthly salary.

For him, knowing that he qualified was enough. It instilled in him the feeling that he was a superman who could achieve anything once he set his mind to it. He defines it as the life-altering moment that helped him to coin his most famous mantra: leaders are those who know how to make the impossible possible.

5

In Search Of Stability

In the seventies, the job market in India was far less complex. People had clear-cut careers with linear growth to choose from. The job one opted for tended to be a reflection of one's education, family background, risk-taking ability and appetite for change. For example, a trader would remain localised, selling his wares all his life from the shop that he had inherited or built. He would have no grand plans to expand his presence across India or diversify the products he was offering customers. It was a manufacturing economy, largely centred on setting up factories and producing everything from Ambassador cars to the wheels they ran on. An industrialist rarely ever diversified his or her manufacturing capability. The white collar worker meanwhile only dreamt of rising to the top of the organisation she/he had joined soon after graduation. Loyalty was the norm and changing jobs was viewed as an act of over ambition.

In this predictable scenario, a government job was coveted since it promised financial security and other guaranteed job benefits. The common consensus was that while private sector jobs might give you wings, a government job gave you deep roots. This sounded like music to the ears of families like Jagdish's who had left everything they owned behind to take refuge in independent India. In their disrupted lives, rootedness felt as precious as gold.

Families like Jagdish's who had managed to flee alive from Pakistan in 1947 wanted to feel the reassuring touch of stability. This meant they either chose to work for Indian blue chip companies run by industrialists' families, or as government employees, joining the armed forces, the administrative services, or being recruited in the many manufacturing units run at the central or state level by the government, or teaching in state-run schools and colleges.

Jagdish too was advised by his brothers to get a government job and find life-long stability. After being refused confirmation at Hans Raj Model School, Jagdish was convinced that he no longer wanted to be at the mercy of private organisations helmed by leaders who played favourites and linked promotions to sycophancy. So, he joined the Directorate of Education, Delhi Government as a teacher of Botany to Senior School students.

On resigning from Hans Raj Model School, the carrot of the corner office and possible principalhood was dangled in front of him by the management. It was suggested that he should stay back and be part of the growth the Trust envisioned for the school. He was also informed that the decision to join the government was unwise as he would hate the rot that was characteristic of government-run schools where education is free, largely attracting students from the lower strata of society who they claimed were a challenge to teach in terms of both discipline and learning ability.

Jagdish, on the contrary, was thrilled to be called for an interview. He was a seasoned player in government-driven education, having availed of it himself up to his graduation. He had witnessed the rot first hand and was not daunted by it. Instead he saw it as his chance to create many more Prabhu Dayals, Jai Dayals and Jagdish Chands. An opportunity to change lives for good.

He had applied for the post a long time ago and this seemed such an opportune moment to get the appointment letter. Jagdish was selected for the job and in 1974, he began a career in government schools, reporting to Government Boys Senior Secondary School, Link Road, Karol Bagh, Delhi. It is a single shift day school, English and Hindi medium, with Classes from 6 to12.

Jagdish's stint with government schools, which lasted for nineteen long years, was ridden with struggle, yet gratifying. During this period, he also added a Bachelors degree in Education (BEd) to his qualifications. The degree was mandated for a government job, but Jagdish had no time to study for it. So, he landed in Jammu for the final exams, totally unprepared. All he had for support were some test prep books with a condensed syllabus and key questions. Interestingly, his roommate, also a biology teacher, was as unprepared. The two came up with a solution: one of them would read the books all day and memorise the subject, verbally revising it before the other as they walked around the city after dinner. Miraculously, the experiment worked and both passed the exam.

~

"When you already have a cushioned platform to kick start your life from, you take the ones who taught you to fly for granted," says Jagdish. "Students from marginalised sections of society have little to fall back on. I find them to be much more sensitive towards the role a guru (teacher) plays in the life of a shishya (student) and follow the guru mantra with much more reverence."

Jagdish is a teacher who calls a smiling student his "real source of vitamins." With immense pride, he shares the story of how he went on to hire a student he had taught in Vaish College as the CEO of Aakash Healthcare and how the student, now a seasoned doctor with an enviable career, had bowed down and touched his feet the moment he recognised Chaudhary Sir who was seated in the Chairman's seat. He recalls the joy he felt when he visited the coaching schools of Vivek Tyagi, a student he had taught biology to at the Link Road School. Tyagi, who belonged to a financially backward background, had built a small empire of his own. Tyagi gave Chaudhary Sir a guided tour of his institution. At that moment, the Guru recalls his heart swelling with pride.

Jagdish has always respected those who manage to be in control of their lives despite the odds. Especially those who turn adversity into enterprise. The stories of such people form the basis of one of his management mantras: necessity is the mother of all business inventions. He vividly remembers the story of one of his students at the Link Road school. The boy was bright and committed to his education. He was, however, always late to class on Saturdays, and the authorities noticed that. Jagdish was asked to take disciplinary action against him. His instincts told him to take the boy aside and ask him the reason gently first. The boy's answer melted his heart immediately.

The boy was the sole breadwinner for his family of seven. He had discovered an ingenuous way to earn enough money at one go for the whole week. Every Saturday, on his way to school, he would place a series of karmandals (copper vessels) filled with mustard oil under trees, traffic lights and at zebra crossings. Every evening he would collect them, this time, filled with coins. Amused as well as perturbed, Jagdish asked his student how he ensured that no one ran away with the vessel filled with cooking-quality mustard oil. The student assured him that no one would have the guts to cross swords with Shani Dev (Saturn), one of the most dreaded gods who is depicted in the Puranas as the God of Karma (deeds), justice and retribution. Devout Hindus believe that this God ensures good actions yield good results and vice versa.

Jagdish went on to take an active interest in his student's life. He was an exception though. Less populated in the mid seventies, government schools were trapped in a vicious cycle of neglect.

Jagdish was appalled to see that the faculty was least interested in teaching. Instead, they were busy trying to make ends meet or simply satisfied with their complacency. Teaching was for them a mere job and they expected classroom the students to learn the subject by rote, parrotlike. Any slip would be met with a lashing. The students were also not serious about academics, which reflected in their results. Schools lacked basic amenities like clean toilets, fans, windows and ventilation. It was as if this realm of schooling did not exist in the mind space of the world.

Jagdish, however, had learnt the art of blossoming wherever he was planted like a lotus. To begin with, he ensured that he kept his classes compelling and informative. He taught students with great enthusiasm, getting them involved, interested in and intrigued by science.

This need to 'engage' the students remains the corner stone of his teaching philosophy, which has been passed on to every teacher at Aakash. In all his institutes, the teachers are forbidden to step into class even with as much as a scrap of paper in their hands as notes. They are expected to know their subject thoroughly and teach it in an engaging manner. For Jagdish, teaching is like therapy. No matter how big his troubles and how high the stress level, seeing a smile on his students' faces makes it all vanish. And the purist in him is also known to stop teaching if he feels his class is not paying full attention or enjoying every second of his session.

He never tires of telling the tale of how he taught a hundred-hour syllabus in ten days. While teaching in Moti Nagar he was asked by the Principal of the government school in Rajouri Garden to substitute for the Biology teacher who was on leave. He was requested to come to the school thrice a week and complete sixty five chapters over four months. For this, he was promised a sum of Rs. 250 per month from the parent-teacher fund which came up to one thousand rupees for the four months.

Jagdish did a quick calculation and realised he would spend all the money on his commute. He was quick to suggest that instead he should be allowed to condense the classes into ten sessions of ten hours each, to be held over the next ten days. The Principal thought he was insane. It would be impossible to keep the students attentive and interested for that long. Jagdish was confident that he could. He even suggested that if any student felt bored, he was free to raise his hand in class. Even if one child did that, Jagdish would stop teaching immediately. For ten days, ten hours each, he taught Biology to Class 12 students. Not even one student raised his or her hand to suggest the class be dismissed!

Calculations like these stemmed from the fact that making ends meet was a constant struggle for Jagdish. He says that he spent two-thirds of his life struggling to give his family a decent life, an education to his sons, and comforts to his wife who never complained. Right up to 1978 he lived in a joint family with his brother Jai and was embarrassed at his meagre contribution to the family's monthly budget. Jai, who was teaching Maths at Bharatiya Vidya Bhawan secured many more tuitions than Jagdish since Maths was a relatively tougher subject than Biology.

It was this need to contribute that triggered Jagdish's first tryst with entrepreneurship. His first partnership was with a fellow teacher who taught Maths to Secondary classes. Alas, it was short-lived and fairly myopic in its mission.

He founded the N.C. Chaudhry Tutor Bureau at a garage in Masjid Moth, in the heart of South Delhi, where he felt there was more demand for tutorials. The two partners took the garage on rent, invested in three chairs and one table, printed leaflets and pasted them all over the affluent colonies in the area. They even placed some in the newspapers. The phone number on the leaflet was of the kirana shop next door and the owner was promised 25 paisa for every call he took on their behalf. The phone rang, once, twice, thrice and many times over. The requisite number of tuitions was elicited. But the enterprise shut down quickly and the partners parted ways. Jagdish kept the chairs and his friend took the table. The capital investment was shared fair and square. From then on, giving tuitions became the means to buffer his small salary. It took on even more importance once he married Kamla.

"My wife is my biggest inspiration, my backbone," says Jagdish. "Her name, Kamla, is one of the many names of Maa Vaishno Devi, and I am Jagdish, 'God' in Hindi. Between us rests our entire mystical world." A Director in Aakash Educational Services Limited, Kamla, a mother and home maker, has stood shoulder to shoulder with Jagdish throughout. She never demanded what was most precious and rare for him: time.

Their story began when Jagdish was 'conned' into meeting Kamla. In 1977 he was residing in a rented apartment with his brother's family in Sriniwaspuri. One day, his landlord suggested they drive to Faridabad together to meet a family friend. It was just a 'casual' outing. Jagdish reached Kamla's house, dressed casually in a T-shirt and he was suddenly asked what he thought of the girl! Jagdish caught on and joked that had he been informed he was 'seeing' a girl, he would have dressed better. He liked her. She approved of him. The deal was done.

Kamla foresaw a life of "middle-class stability" with Jagdish. A case of "two teachers who would earn a decent living, enjoy a stable life and also have time to go on holiday together as a family." She says, "The day I first met him he struck me as an intelligent man with whom I would be able to build a good life." She also remembers that he was a tad bit too casually dressed for the occasion of "seeing a girl as a prospective wife."

Her life with Jagdish proved to be anything but stable. Kamla has had the grit and patience to stand steadfast through her family's many ups and downs. The day she said yes in sync with Jagdish's yes, a synchronicity was born and it has been reflected in all their joint decisions through the years.

The shagun (pre-wedding ceremony to cement the liaison) date was fixed. When Kamla's parents came to Jagdish's home for the engagement ceremony, there was no pundit to be found. The tech savvy Jagdish found a solution. He played the Gayatri Mantra on his tape recorder and received the shagun—the auspicious coconut.

The wedding three months later was no different. It was simple, cost effective and quick. Jagdish told his father categorically that he was not going to take loans and burden himself. All he had was Rs. 1500. He was willing to borrow Rs. 6000 from a cousin who worked for DCM (Delhi Cloth Mill) for a reception post-marriage, but most for the marriage. His father Nanak Chand was upset at this frugality. He was worried about his biradari (extended family) and duniyadaari (social norms). Jagdish insisted that he would require no baraat (procession), no histrionics, elaborate tents, lighting, floral arrangements and other paraphernalia. He reached Kamla's house at noon and by four in the afternoon they were on their way back, the girl sitting next to him in his uncle's car now his wife.

The next day, the couple took off to Jammu and Kashmir with their cousin Satya Pal who had also got married recently. Jagdish had no money for his honeymoon, so he requested his eldest brother-in-law, Mr. Gopal Sethi, to give him a loan of Rs. 1500 which he promised pay back in five months from his tuitions. Their first stop was at the Maa Vaishno Devi shrine. Intoxicated with love and the prospect of a shared future, Jagdish was overwhelmed by the vibrations of the shrine. He stood there, transfixed, in the cold cave where the Goddess had merged her human form with the astral form of her creators, the three supreme energies: Maa Vaishno, Maa Kali and Maa Laxmi. This trip became a yearly ritual for the family and it continues to this day.

From Katra, they boarded a bus to Srinagar. A picturesque ride across winding roads filled with Himalayan views later, they reached their hotel. It was day one of their fifteen-day break and Jagdish decided to flag it off by seeing his favourite hero, Amitabh's blockbuster movie, *Amar Akbar Anthony* with his wife. But when the two returned after the late-night show at 1.15 a.m., the hotel was in total darkness, the doors locked. The prospect of spending their first night together on the cold, desolate road scared them. They banged on the front door desperately. Many suspenseful moments later the door was unlatched and they crossed the threshold and entered a new life together...One that was going to be a great roller coaster for both.

The same year Jagdish and Kamla rented a barsaati (one-room apartment) at New Rohtak Road, Delhi. The place was so small that after they placed a double bed in it, there was little space to move around. In fact, the landlady on showing them the flat, was skeptical if any 'sane' wife would like to make this tiny hole her first home with her newly-wed husband. To this, Jagdish gave one of his famous, distracted remarks. Says Kamla, "He told her that his wife was a dehati (villager) with few opinions of her own and wouldn't mind it! Later, when I made friends with the landlady she said that that I was anything but a woman with no opinions. I thought about how Jagdish, the one who came from a distant village, had branded me a villager. This incident has remained a joke among us ever since."

After about four months, they shifted to a double storey flat in West Patel Nagar. It was in this home that the Chaudhry boys were born. On 11 August, 1978 the two were blessed with their first born, Aashish and on 11 September, 1979, along came Aakash. Their sky was filled with stars and the young man who treated a trip to Connaught Place as his life's goal was now a husband and a proud father of two.

Aashish's arrival was a moment of joy underlined with shock and grief. The boy had clubfeet and the parents felt helpless at first. Then, they consulted several orthopedic surgeons who were experts in pediatrics. They were counselled to tie a tight bandage on the baby's feet. Aashish was bandaged and thereafter ensued a spate of consultations with doctors, a series of operations and medical expenses that turned Jagdish into a tuition machine. Aashish shares an incident that offers deep insight into how his father relied on his instincts at this time. When he went to consult the surgeons at Safdarjung Hospital for Aashish's surgery, he saw Mr. Bhatura, a classmate from his BSc Final days in Gurgaon whom he deeply admired for the precision with which he used to dissect the arteries of a pigeon in the Biology lab. He was convinced of his surgical acumen and chose him to operate on Aashish over the head of department. His instincts were right and Aashish's club feet became a thing of the past.

Many years later, Jagdish once again relied on a young surgeon whom he believed in for his own knee surgery. The surgeon was his son Aashish, who had just flagged off Aakash Healthcare in Delhi's emerging suburb Dwarka, and was very tense about the prospect of inaugurating the surgery facility with an operation on the Chairman's knees. "It was a make or break moment for our reputation," recalls Aashish. Despite his nervousness, the operation was successful and went on to catapult the hospital to fame.

~

Jagdish taught round the clock when his sons were young. His days were full; teaching, giving one-on-one tuitions to Senior Secondary students, and writing textbooks which were part of the CBSE syllabus. His books were a teacher's best friend, explaining complex subjects in a simple way. A busy man, he never attended PTSMA meetings in his son's school. One day, he noticed that Aashish was being taught a certain topic in Biology wrong. When he talked about this to Aashish, his answer was predictably that of a student in awe of his teacher. Jagdish attended the PTSMA meeting and spoke to the teacher concerned. To his surprise, she said that she had read it in J.C. Chaudhry's book! After the matter was sorted out, Aashish was in total awe of his father.

Only allowing himself a few hours of sleep, Jagdish usually left home early in the morning when his children were sleeping, and returned after they had gone to bed. His greatest regret was that he could not find time for them. The boys only saw their father rush in and out of the house or give tutorials in his makeshift classroom upstairs. Aakash remembers how shocked he was when his father rushed him to the hospital after he hurt himself while playing a game with Aashish. "He was giving a tutorial upstairs. When he saw how hurt I was, he dropped his chalk, dismissed the class, grabbed me and rushed me to the hospital. I was shocked to realise that he actually cared for us."

Jagdish did care deeply for his family. When Aashish was a baby, he was severely dehydrated one day and a bout of vomiting and food poisoning turned him as pale as chalk. A family friend, Mrs. Uppal, told the young couple to rush him to the hospital. Jagdish had a class waiting so he admitted his son to the hospital and rushed back to class. While he was teaching, he saw his wife returning in a three-wheeler with a neighbour. Aashish was lying on her lap, all wrapped up. "His heart sank and he thought of the worst," says Aashish. "But we were coming home after receiving treatment and I was on the road to recovery." Work-life balance was a tough challenge for Jagdish, but he tried his best to find it for the sake of his wife and children.

Helping him whole heartedly in this balancing act was Kamla, a teacher who became a housewife the moment Aashish was born with the underlying health issue of club feet. She sensed that while Jagdish's life was totally consumed by his work, she had to make herself available to her sons at all times. A grandmother and a mother-in-law today, she feels that her parenting mantra is practise patience and be a true friend to her children. "Their father was always busy. And, while he took a keen interest in their studies and was instrumental in leading them to the right academic path, it was I who became their friend...Someone they felt comfortable to confide in."

For most part of his teaching life, Jagdish struggled. The good phase finally arrived when he wore a blue sapphire ring on his finger.

The gemologist in him attributes his first step towards prosperity to an incident. Sitting in a classroom that he shared with a colleague, he rued how even though he had worked for sixteen years, he could ill afford a hut, leave alone a home. His heart was questioning his fate as he wondered if the next sixty years would be similar. His colleague, a believer in the power of gem stones had been advised to wear blue sapphire, a precious stone known to influence one's fate, for good or bad.

Jagdish too bought one with great trepidation, kept it under his pillow and started wearing it after three days. Interestingly, he saw instant results. Within a few days, he was asked to start his own coaching class by the Principal of Bal Bharati School, a friend who promised to help him find his first six students too. A classroom was created at the dining table of the Chaudhrys' home. His fame as a teacher had travelled far and wide and this step was the first in a series of successes. He has never looked back since then and refers to this as the *Geet Gaya Pathron Ne* moment in his life, linking the blue sapphire to the classic movie directed by V. Shantaram.

Jagdish's stint of teaching in government schools lasted from 1974 to 1993. He taught in the school at Link Road for four years, moving to the Government Sarvodaya Senior Secondary School, Moti Nagar in 1977. He taught there up to 1987 and then moved to Vikaspuri District Centre where he worked till 1992. His swan song with Delhi Government schools was as Principal after being selected by the Union Public Service Commission (UPSC) for the post.

His interview for the post of Principal was an eventful one. Jagdish was laid up in bed with a slip disc when he got the call. He convinced two of his cousins to accompany him for the interview. They carried him to their car and made him lie down flat in the rear seat. This is how he was driven to the interview, down but not out. His cousins also ferried him into the room where the interview panel was seated, and placed him on a chair in front of the members. Shocked, the panel asked him why he had come all the way when he was evidently in the throes of pain. Smiling, he replied that he did not want to deny them the opportunity of hiring a great Principal who was 100% committed to his job.

Jagdish was promoted to the post and sent as Principal to Government Sarvodaya Bal Vidyalaya, Matiala. During his memorable stint there he brought about hundred positive changes to the school, which gave the institution the reputation of being a 'model' school thereafter. From improving the teacher-student ratio to bettering the sanitation facilities to creating lush gardens and motivating students to do better at their studies, Jagdish's contribution to the school's growth was immense.

Politics and groupism were the biggest hurdles he faced there. A by-product of red tape and bureaucracy, politics had seeped into most government departments. This was unacceptable to Jagdish. He tried his best to steer clear of political camps and petty rivalries on campus. Never once was he accused of picking personal favourites among the teachers. Practical, driven and straightforward, he was a 'what you see is what you get' sort of Principal.

After his successful tenure at the school, Chaudhry Sir finally handed in his resignation in October 1994. He was all set to become the legendary entrepreneur J.C. Chaudhry who would transform the test-prep market for good with Aakash Institute.

6

An Entrepreneur Is Born

Among the many inspiring stories that Jagdish often shares with people is the one about how Thomas Alva Edison discovered the light bulb after a thousand failed experiments. Edison was so focused on work that he once locked himself and his team up in the laboratory in order to finish a task. No amount of pleading by his assistants worked. Their spouses had to sneak in food and other necessities into the laboratory to keep them going!

Aakash Institute was Jagdish's 'light bulb moment'. Like most significant discoveries, it came into being after many failed attempts. It demanded hard work, relentless struggle and the courage to face many letdowns. D.N. Taneja, a close friend and associate of Jagdish's, recites a famous verse by Allama Iqbal. "These lines aptly describe my friend who never gives up," says Taneja.

Hazaron saal nargis apni benoori pe roti hai
Badi mushkil se hota hai chaman mein deedavar paida
(For a thousand years the narcissus flower laments its blindness;
Till one day a brave soul with a vision is born and the garden blooms again.)

Many who are stuck at the deep end of a tunnel are well aware of the light at the end; yet, they prefer to hide in the false safety of the dark, rather than facing life and getting to the end of the tunnel. Jagdish, however, had the guts to brave it out, blooming like the brave narcissus in Iqbal's poem. A teacher at heart, he also has the brain and brawn of an entrepreneur. He had the vision to monetise his teaching skills and turn his gift into a business opportunity. Before he had the Eureka moment with Aakash Institute, he had made more than one attempt to set up various educational ventures. His first attempt in 1977—N.C. Chaudhry Tutor Bureau—ended as quickly as it began.

In 1982, he founded Aashish College of Correspondence, his attempt number two at entrepreneurship. Based on a long-distance support model, the 'College' comprised of a team of three teachers, including Chaudhry Sir. He and his team created sample test papers along with the answers for final year students. This innovation came about when the demand could not meet the supply. Jagdish's classes were packed and despite teaching like a 'machine' he could not close the need gap. So, he decided to offer a correspondence course and prepare well-written notes for science students.

While he was able to create the papers for Botany and Zoology himself, A.D. Taneja, his guide and mentor since his BITS Pilani days, agreed to create preparatory notes for Chemistry. Jagdish enlisted the support of another trusted teacher to prepare the papers for Physics and Mathematics. Every week, the three would get their papers ready. Jagdish would take these hand-written notes to Usha, a stenographer he had hired. Sitting in his makeshift office at his home, Usha would type all day. Jagdish would then painstakingly photocopy all the notes on a Gestetner cyclostyling machine he had bought for Rs. 1500. Kamla stapled these notes together and got them ready for dispatch.

"On the surface I was just playing his assistant, but as a couple we were in the struggle together. I knew my husband was working beyond his mental and physical means. Hence, every bit of support I could give made me feel that I was helping him in his Herculean act," says Kamla. Being an academic herself, Kamla could understand the world of coaching perfectly.

Jagdish and his faithful lab assistant Hari Chand went door to door, dropping the notes off to students. Hari was paid 25 paisa per drop. He would pretend to be the peon at the 'College' telling everyone that Chaudhry Sir did not trust courier companies and had sent him to drop off the papers personally. Little did they know that Chaudhry Sir's scooter was parked right outside their homes!

This process continued for a few months, turning Jagdish's daily working hours from ten to fifteen. From 4 to 6.30 a.m. he would give tuitions at Chanakyapuri, which was far away from his school and residence. By 7 a.m., he would rush back to school where he would continue to work till 2 p.m. Thereafter came a series of tuitions that kept him busy till 8 p.m.

It became even tougher when Taneja fell sick and the Physics teacher started arm-twisting him to be paid more. Instead of giving in, Jagdish took matters into his own hands. He drove to Nai Sadak (the hub for textbooks and educational material in Old Delhi), bought Maths, Physics and Chemistry textbooks, and started writing all the notes himself. As a result, he was able to afford only three hours of sleep every night from then on.

He had no time to shave or eat a proper meal. His body ached with fatigue. Sleep deprived and over worked, he decided to unwind with Chandra Bhan Thanai, a lawyer friend of his who suggested they meet and spend some time together. In the good old days, the two friends would catch up every fortnight over drinks and dinner. But when Jagdish rang his doorbell unannounced in the evening, Thanai did not recognise the weary soul. Thanai was shocked and reprimanded Jagdish for working himself to death. He warned his friend that that if he continued on this path, he would burn out soon.

That night, things changed dramatically. Jagdish made a spur-of-the-moment choice. At midnight, when he reached home after having dinner with Thanai, he woke up Kamla, brought out all the photocopied notes, the banners of Aashish College of Correspondence, his books and stationery, and lit a bonfire with them! Kamla kept requesting him to wait till the morning. However, Jagdish knew he had to end this before it ended him. The deed was done. The next day was a new dawn for the brave entrepreneur.

"I believe in taking quick, instinctive decisions. It is better to cut the cord in life than to endure the pain," says Jagdish. There are many instances in the past when he chose to take bold steps on his own without overthinking his decisions. He remembers the incident of selling off an old Vespa scooter—jointly bought by him and his big brother Jai in 1976. They had spent Rs. 1600 each on the vehicle, but the second-hand Vespa was unpredictable and would stop on a whim, embarrassing the brothers in public. Jagdish was so petrified of being let down that when he drove his wife to her maternal home on the weekends, he would stay up the night before, worrying about his scooter and how it would humiliate him before his in-laws.

The brothers took turns to ride it. Odd days were his and even ones his brother Jai's. Once, when Jagdish was going to the market to buy vegetables, the stubborn scooter stopped in its tracks. Something inside his head snapped. He kick started it and drove it straight to the mechanic's shop, selling it at half the price, merely three months after having bought it. Then, he spent the money from the sale on a tape recorder, two T-shirts and gifts for the children and Kamla before taking a bus to his brother's school in Lutyens Delhi. He handed over Jai's share of Rs. 800 to him. Jai was bewildered as well as a bit amused. He knew that for Jagdish, it was simply a case of deed done, matter closed.

Jagdish calls this his idea of 'doing something', a phrase he coined as a teacher to help students and colleagues to 'decide fast' and rid themselves of the apathy and fear that had made them immobile for years. He noticed that even a minor act or decision taken quickly inspired them. His decision to quit his job in 1994 and work for his wife's educational venture, Aakash Institute, stemmed from this theory of "doing something."

~

Seeing her husband turn into a highly sought after coach and also troubled by his struggle to travel from one coaching class to the other,

Kamla founded Aakash Institute on 22 September, 1988 at A-38, Ganesh Nagar in West Delhi. This was their first medical entrance coaching centre. At the start, the Institute chose to only coach students preparing for AIPMT (All India Pre-Medical Test), which was a conscious decision since Jagdish was a master of half the course for AIPMT. He ensured his students mastered the syllabus of Botany and Zoology, the two subjects that he taught.

Jagdish was still employed as a school teacher when Kamla set up the Institute. He sought permission to step in and support his wife's venture without taking any charges. A qualified teacher who had opted to play the role of mother, guide and nurturer to her sons, Kamla understood the business of teaching and proved to be an astute, hard-working businesswoman. She was in charge of the Institute's administration. She has always been Jagdish's pillar of strength, his rock of Gibraltar, truly his 'better half' in every sense.

By 1990, Aakash Institute started showing results. Students queued up to study there and in response, a second centre at B-35, Ganesh Nagar was launched. In 1993, the Institute had its 'no looking back moment' when twenty three students were selected in Delhi PMT, the maximum count by a single coaching centre in Delhi. Jagdish resigned from his job the next year, unbuckling his safety belt and taking the car off cruise control. Quitting the stable job was his move to 'do something', to take a bold step forward. It was time for him to soar into the wide open sky. For a buoyant Jagdish, even the sky did not look like the limit. And he was amply rewarded for his bold decision soon. In 1994, Aakash Institute produced a first rank holder in Delhi PMT and Chaudhry Sir's happiness knew no bounds.

By 2000, Aakash Institute was a well-established brand in the test-prep market for AIPMT, bagging the number one position in industry reviews and media surveys. Consistently maintaining this lead, they conquered the Delhi market and established their mettle in giving good results. So spectacular was the results that Aakash Institute was booking eight-page advertisements to accommodate all the students who were admitted to medical colleges of repute. "That was the peak of his stardom as a teacher. He was being seen as a magician who gave results. Every parent wanted their child to study at Aakash and train under him," shares Aakash. Jagdish's innovative paradigm of coaching, up-to-date course material and his ability to ensure that every teacher at Aakash taught with utmost dedication were making the country sit up and take notice.

Instead of resigning from his government job, Jagdish could have stayed a school teacher all his life and moved up the ladder to be a principal. This would have ensured a steady monthly income and he would still have been considered a success in the eyes of the world. Given his humble beginnings, it would have been commendable enough if he rose to the position of principal of a full-fledged Senior Secondary school in Delhi. But he was never one to play safe and steer clear of risks.

A shocker awaited him when he retired from his job though. At the time of leaving the school, he had accumulated two lakh rupees as PF and gratuity and decided to invest it in a plot in Gurgaon. He had secured the land at a reduced price under the ministerial quota. The dream of owning a home was about to finally come true. The Chaudhrys were thrilled. They had used their hard-earned money wisely. Fate, however, had different plans for them. By a stroke of bad luck, the ministerial quota was cancelled and Jagdish lost the entire sum.

On hearing the news, he went into deep shock. Gripped by grief, he felt dizzy and he fainted. He was rushed to Rajinder Nagar for treatment. There, he was placed under the care of a VIP doctor whose son he had admitted to his Institute just a day before. The grateful doctor had promised to take care of Jagdish's medical needs. On seeing Jagdish take up that offer so quickly, the doctor joked with Kamla that her husband knew how to 'encash' a favour quickly!

Though crestfallen, Jagdish called this his second innings. He consoled himself by citing a book he had read wherein the protagonist loses all his possessions in a fire. Unfazed, he called it an opportunity to bid goodbye to every bad turn his life had taken so far. Jagdish the entrepreneur was born with a clean slate. Free, not answerable to anyone but himself and his God. He had no liabilities since he owned nothing except the will to conquer the world and teach to his heart's content. He was confident about changing the way the world viewed the emerging test-prep market.

~

AIPMT (All India Pre-Medical Test) conducted by the Central Board of Secondary Education (CBSE) was introduced in 1988. Admissions to most medical colleges became linked to this entrance exam. Students no longer had to appear for a series of localised entrance exams except if they wanted to get admission in AIIMS that continues to select candidates on the basis of a separate entrance exam. AIPMT is a requirement for admission to MBBS and BDS degree programmes in several medical colleges across the country. 15% of the seats in all medical and dental colleges run by the Government of India, state governments, municipal or other local bodies, except in Andhra Pradesh, Telangana and Jammu and Kashmir, were reserved for candidates who qualified in this examination.

The Indian medical education system is one of the largest in the world. The number of medical colleges in India has rapidly proliferated in the past twenty five years, doubling since 1980. Those who want to be doctors prepare for the entrance test with singular focus. Many aspirants drop out of college for years on end to take the entrance exam multiple times in the hope of making it. The move to centralise the exam allowed students more choice of colleges, but it also meant that they were putting all their eggs in one basket. The pressure of appearing for this crucial test built up soon after they finished their Board exams. This called for genius coupled with hard work. The multiple-choice format demanded that the aspirants have a deep understanding of the subjects. The need to score high in the exam made many students rely on the crutches of coaching. This trend gave rise to the birth of several coaching schools. Ambitious parents reached out to reputed teachers and were ready to pay teachers handsomely to ensure seats for their children in the prestigious medical colleges of India.

For Jagdish, it was always about teaching well, helping the students to fall in love with the subject and appear for the entrance exam with a mind that was free of doubts. In his classes there two sets of blinkered horses: the teacher who wanted to teach the subject well and the students who only thought about clearing the exam and getting into a good medical college. Everything else was forgotten. Worldly worries like heat, lack of ventilation and birdcagelike classrooms did not bother the guru or the shishya.

Jagdish smiles when he talks about how the roof of the first centre in Ganesh Nagar was so low and the room so badly ventilated that every other week a student would faint due to the heat. Jagdish would personally drop the student home. The next day, both would be back in class, the previous day's incident forgotten!

Jagdish attributes the success of his students not just to the quality of teaching that he has always maintained, but also to the sense of motivation that he feels is like a tonic for the mind. The student must be motivated or else the teacher's efforts will fail. "No matter how hard a teacher may try, a de-motivated mind will not let anything seep in."

Jagdish puts classroom experience above any corporate mantra or marketing theory. Ask him what his corporate philosophy is and he says it is all about feeling the celestial song when in class. Connecting with the heart of each student and answering all their doubts, he makes sure students develop a deep understanding of subjects. To him, it is vital that teachers feel the fire in their bellies and teach well. Everything else ceases to matter.

He says that democracy without education is nothing but a facade. His dream is to create what he calls a 'pool of talented teachers'. He feels that a good teacher should put his job before anything else. It is imperative that she/he should not be caught up in worldly matters or be saddled with the worry of making ends meet.

Jagdish believes that it is the State's responsibility to create a pool of great teachers. All you need to begin with is one 'perfect teacher' with a magical teaching style. The government could handpick one such genius in each state through a centralised entrance exam. This genius should be further trained to master the art of educating children to be aware and intelligent citizens. They could also train other teachers to follow their footsteps. Once this 'army' of great teachers step into the classroom, they will mould students' minds like a potter shapes wet clay, guiding them in the right direction, ensuring they are well educated, not just understanding their subjects but also possibly loving it.

Jagdish the educationist laments the lack of true education in India, which rests on research, invention and development. As the Chairman of Aakash Healthcare, whenever he attends overseas medical fairs to procure the latest machinery, it breaks his heart to see Indian manufacturing capability lagging so far behind. "Germany, France, Russia, all invest billions in research. Most scientists in the United States are Indians. Yet, we have nothing in the name of indigenous production here," he says. "If our scientists get their due, if we celebrate pure sciences, if the government invests enough energy in invention, then the next generation of science students will not need to take up a job. They can become entrepreneurs and mass produce their inventions. This will elevate the available technology in every sphere of our lives."

To make the nation self-sufficient in terms of research ability and at par with the rest of the world—this to him is the true goal of education. He talks of self-sufficient India, unwittingly echoing the current government's mantra, 'Atmanirbhar Bharat'. However, it is not his intention to espouse any political theories or parrot a political party's manifesto. He is convinced that education must be totally divorced from politics. The only significant role a government can perform is in helping to multiply the number of educational institutes in the country.

This visionary educationist also explains that doubling the number of hospitals and colleges in India will halt the brain drain. For him, it is easier to respect a doctor who goes back to his or her village to serve their people, rather than work in a hospital abroad. He shares the story of one of his gifted students from Lucknow who cleared the entrance exam at AIIMS after two tries. He reached out to Chaudhry Sir for help since he could not afford the monthly hostel fee of five thousand rupees. Instantly recalling the role Taneja had played in helping him at BITS Pilani, Jagdish offered to pay the fee from his personal funds for four-and-a-half years.

Touched, thrilled and humbled, the student promised to make Aakash Institute and Jagdish proud. To the guru's dismay, however, the student was spotted a few years later on a television show talking of his coaching business in a far-flung area of Uttar Pradesh. Jagdish called him and jokingly asked him why he was becoming a competitor to an educational institute that had supported him. His student's answer touched Jagdish to the core. He said that either he could be a doctor and serve his people in the village or help create a battery of doctors from these remote regions of the country who would then return and serve a much larger number of people. In his own way, this Aakashian was a catalyst, trying to create a pool of excellent doctors who would make their remote villages self-reliant in terms of their medical needs.

7

Aakash–From Institute To Enterprise

1988–2000

Focused and disciplined, Jagdish moved steadily towards his goal. Aakash Institute had to become not just a profitable business but also one that transformed lives by helping students from every strata of society realise their dreams. Jagdish worked day and night to turn his dream into reality. This hardworking and innovative entrepreneur was also blessed with the ability to infuse life into the most boring of subjects and inspire his students to delve deep into them.

In a span of six years (1988–1994), Aakash Institute had three centres to its credit with the demand for classes and teachers growing by the day. The Institute's fame was spreading far and wide and good results were pouring in. All that was needed now was a first rank, a topper to place the cherry on top of the well-iced cake. This happened in 1996 when a student who had enrolled for the crash course in March secured first rank in the AIPMT exam. With this win, Aakash Institute gained national acclaim. The Institute had succeeded in building a formidable reputation for itself in the field of test prep.

"Parents started to believe that toppers are made only at Aakash Institute," says Aashish. "They wanted their children to study there under the direct tutelage of Chaudhry Sir. My father met this demand with great gusto. He was like a tiger, feisty, springing up to take on any challenge that came his way." Jagdish continued to teach all day at school and coach batches of students at Aakash right up to his retirement.

Aakash Institute was now a full-fledged, profitable and meaningful enterprise. Like most coaching centres helmed by educators, the Institute had started as a simple home-tuition operation set up by a much sought after teacher who wanted to add to his monthly income. With increasing demand, it moved on to group tuitions. This transition came about because of the need to make the burgeoning demand meet the limited supply of an incredible teacher: Chaudhry Sir. The Biology teacher taught so engagingly that all doubts vanished and his students attained a crystal-clear mental state.

Aakash Institute was destined for glory. The next milestone it reached was the launch of coaching classes for the entire spectrum of pure sciences including Physics and Chemistry. Aakash had entered its next phase of growth. The highly effective coaching classes produced excellent results. Many students were selected to prestigious colleges such as AIIMS, Maulana Azad Medical College, New Delhi Christian Medical College, Vellore, etc.

Jagdish's venture had grown into a respected institution with an address, a building where classes were conducted and a small batch of teachers who were handpicked by him. Jagdish is a visionary who has a gift to spot committed teachers from a mile away. All the credit for turning the Institute into a flourishing enterprise goes to Jagdish. He saw merit in structure and organisation and invested wisely in the crucial elements that are make or break for the test-prep business: good teachers, a structured syllabus, engaging classes and well-researched, meticulously prepared notes for the students to take home. He also made sure to constantly upgrade all the facilities at the Institute. Even when he had very little money, this educator/entrepreneur had the ability to think big. He overcame many hurdles and stayed focused on building an organisation based on the management mantras of success and delivery.

Hailing from a generation that believes in growing slowly, steadily and honestly, Jagdish preferred to keep the most important ingredient of success—quality control, in his hands. Right up to 2003 the focus was on making the home ground, Delhi, strong. The entire city had to be conquered by Aakash with good intent and the conviction of producing results. Franchise was not a word that entered Aakash's vocabulary till nine years after its birth. Even today, the number of self-owned centres is higher than the franchised ones. Though ambitious, the management was not caught up in a frenetic growth mode. Instead, the focus was on creating a brand, shaping lives, and winning accolades for helping the young step into well-defined careers of their choice. Jagdish's midas touch and his dedication to quality control were the basis of all operations.

In 1997, nine years after Aakash Institute came into existence; the first franchise was given to Jagdish's trusted friend and fellow teacher, M.L. Arora. With this, the fourth centre was born in Pandav Nagar. The next year, a student who had enrolled in the classroom course at the Institute secured a first rank in the CBSE (AIPMT/PDT) Final Exam. Thereafter, there was no slipping from the position of 'number one Institute for AIPMT' and subsequently for the National Eligibility cum Entrance Test (NEET), which went on to replace AIPMT. NEET is the single entrance exam for admission to more than 66,000 MBBS and BDS seats across India. As per the NMC Act 2019, NEET-UG became the common all-India entrance exam for premium institutes including AIIMS and Jawaharlal Institute of Postgraduate Medical Education and Research (JIPMER).

Though it had become a household name in west Delhi, Aakash's management wanted to move to south Delhi where aspirations were higher and pockets deeper. The search was launched for a centre in the heart of affluent south Delhi. The perfect address was spotted by accident when Jagdish went shopping to Big Jo's, one of the first multi-brand outlets to enter the high-fashion landscape of India.

Just as he had started to hunt for some formal clothes, he noticed a 'To Let' sign at a prime location in South Extension, right opposite Ring Road that strings the whole city together. He saw the board stamped Jainco, a trusted property dealer of the area, and immediately drove to the site.

Jagdish loved the location the moment he saw it and decided this was it. Instead of shopping for formals, he put down a token advance and booked the building. He had stepped out to buy clothes and ended up buying himself a building—one of the many fabled spur-of-the-moment decisions made by this self-made tycoon during his journey to success.

In 1998, Aakash Institute's first south Delhi address—L-4, South Extension, was inaugurated. Finding their feet in this region was a challenge at the start. The upwardly-mobile, ultra-rich south Delhi denizens were skeptical about sending their children to a 'new' coaching institute with no history to back it up. Besides, the prestigious Sangal Classes located bang opposite Aakash Institute had already proven its mettle in the test prep arena. Fancy cars with fancier people would land up outside Aakash Institute's portals. They would walk in, enquire about the classes, pick up a brochure and walk out.

Soon enough, however, word spread and many students who were driving all the way to Janakpuri or Mahavir Nagar from south and central Delhi started enrolling here. Seats slowly started filling up. After the results were announced that year, new enrollments came pouring in. Jagdish and his team were delighted to welcome them.

In 2000, a second centre was set up at K-11 South Extension. The next year, the second franchise sprung up at Wazirpur, filling the gap in north Delhi. In 2002, a new centre opened at Janakpuri. Eventually, the competition faded away and Aakash towered over the rest in the test-prep market.

The Institute was in high demand with students pouring in from all over the country. The moment they had completed their Board exam, students would rush in to enroll for the crash course. Despite so many centres, the seats at Aakash were filling up fast. With limited seats, it became even more crucial to hand pick the finest students who had the potential to excel and ace the entrance test. A test-prep and coaching institute's reputation and mettle depend entirely on the number of students succeeding in AIPMT, and at getting admission in JIPMER and AIIMS.

As the demand increased, so did the innovation. Aakash Institute introduced innovative preparatory formats that brought their expert facility to many more students. Jagdish introduced a month-long crash course, which crunched the entire syllabus into a power packed thirty days. This helped students from smaller cities and quasi-towns to make their way to Delhi to study at Aakash Institute. Held just before the entrance exams, this format was very effective in preparing the students for the forthcoming entrance test. It charged them up and motivated them to study 24/7, and helped them in revising the entire syllabus. The pioneering first rank holder from Aakash Institute was a crash course student.

Test and Discussion (TAD) was yet another interesting variant they introduced. In this format, students gave a series of mock tests, consulting a senior professor one on one after each test. Discussing their answers threadbare they were able to analyse every point they had missed. This format went a long way in helping students overcome their weaknesses, besides strengthening their strong points.

With the demand for a career in medicine growing, and the number of medical colleges not drastically increasing, the test-prep market became a natural corollary to formal education. It was no longer 'shadow education' as purists liked to call it. Coaching centres like Aakash were constructively enhancing the education experience with their logic-based approach to competitive examinations.

In 2003, Jagdish came up with an ingenious, big idea: hold an entrance test to Aakash Institute, set, conducted and evaluated internally. Only students who made it to the merit list would get a chance to train at India's premium coaching institute. This decision shook up the market. Many thought it was preposterous for a private institute to 'select' students. Nevertheless, the national-level All India Aakash Test Series (AIATS) was launched. And Jagdish learnt yet another crucial lesson: when it becomes tough to enter an institute or course, the aspirants' need to make it gets higher. With AIATS, the Institute decided to look beyond Delhi and opened centres in Guwahati and Ranchi.

The first twelve years, between 1988 and 2000, were turbulent, ridden with troubles and full of shocking ups and downs that could put a roller coaster ride at Disneyworld to shame. This included arm-twisting tactics for pay hikes by some teachers, poaching of students by the competition, devastating tax raids and living in constant fear of a sealing drive. All these experiences were nerve-wracking. They crushed Jagdish's dreams and tested him in the toughest ways. But this self-made entrepreneur was made of tougher mettle.

"The most important ingredient for making an education enterprise a success is that those helming it must be educators themselves. Otherwise they will be cheated and their dreams will be derailed even before they take off. You cannot succeed in this field simply with capital, land you own and a few teachers who you employ. This is an industry best handled by an insider—someone who understands the nuances of teaching," says Jagdish.

When you are a one-man show like him, juggling funds, time and commitment is a constant struggle. There are moments when you feel you are running at full speed and yet stuck to a spot. There have been many obstacles in his path. To his credit, he found innovative way to overcome them and learn from them. He happily shares six valuable mantras he has formulated over the years based on his experience. Fledgling education start-ups can use these to dodge bullets and handle difficult situations.

Mantra 1: Students come first. The bottom line of a coaching institute is the number of students who get admission into colleges and courses of their choice. That is the real profit.

Education is student driven. They are the key ingredient of your story. Students need to believe in you and stick with you. You have to make sure they understand your good intentions or else they will become demotivated and be poached by the competition. Attrition of teachers and poaching of students are very common in this business. This hurts the most when an institute is young and still finding its footing.

Jagdish relives the shock of walking into his Institute one morning to find that one of his Zoology teachers had poached 320 'Aakashians' at one go. It was a loss the fledgling Institute was in no position to take on, both financially and reputationwise.

Chaudhry Sir, the beloved professor, rose to the occasion. He personally invited all the students for a meeting and gave them a long pep talk. He ensured them that Aakash and its well-crafted coaching module was the best route to success. He worked very hard to make them change their minds. In the end, thanks to his power of persuasion, 260 students decided to continue at Aakash. The battle was momentarily won.

Students have always been Jagdish's top priority. However, there have been a few instances when he slipped up. In the early years, when he was busy constructing the third centre at Mahavir Nagar, he would ask one of the other teachers to take over his class. One day, a delegation of disgruntled students came to him. They argued that a new building would be of no use if, in the bargain, they failed their tests and their careers were derailed. Their words hit him hard. From the next day, Chaudhry Sir reclaimed the class. As a symbol of penance he taught his students barefoot. The class was thrilled and touched by his dedication. They begged him to wear his shoes. That year, the Institute went on to deliver spectacular results making both the students and Chaudhry Sir very happy.

In 1998, when the first franchise was launched in Pandav Nagar, the franchisee asked the management to help him to find a good Physics teacher. Vadhera, a trusted and brilliant teacher, was sent there. Within two months, a frantic Arora called up complaining that the Physics teacher had literally 'hypnotised' the students, leading them to his own coaching class, which he had launched at Alcone Public School next door. Immediately, Mishra Sir was sent to replace Vadhera to teach Zoology and motivate the students. Chaudhry Sir joined him every evening, teaching the Botany class with great gusto and bringing most of the poached students back.

He reversed the trend by administering a strong dose of Vitamin M (Motivation).

Jagdish ruled with an iron hand and if he sensed a deficiency of discipline he dealt with it in the toughest manner. The students who were preparing for the entrance exams needed to be like Arjuna, the accomplished archer, with their eyes glued to the target. It is a war and discipline is integral for the win. Jagdish took tough disciplinary action also to keep the toppers on track. He insisted that after every internal test conducted during classes, students attend a session to discuss their paper. The participation of the entire class was compulsory as these sessions highlighted the strengths and weaknesses in each student's prep. Anyone who missed these sessions risked incurring Jagdish's displeasure.

Punctuality was a must in his organisation and overlooking it, a punishable offence. Even a five-minute delay would be enough for a student or teacher to be ordered to miss the class and sit on a bench planted outside the classroom. Just like charity, punctuality begins at home as far as Jagdish is concerned. One day, Aashish who also coached at Aakash for AIPMT, was late to class. He was allowed to sneak in by the timetable keeper. When Jagdish came to know of this, he pulled his son out from the class at once. He was made to sit on the bench along with the other latecomers. No concessions were allowed, not even for his son.

Mantra 2: Never cow down before miscreant staff or give in to vested interests. Bad apples are best thrown out of the basket.

Aakash Educational Services Limited (AESL) had its fair share of trouble in terms of retaining teachers in the initial years. Poaching is rampant in the competitive field of test prep. In 2004, a leading coaching school from south India opened a centre each bang opposite Aakash Institute's South Extension and Janakpuri centres in Delhi. Quietly and surreptitiously, in the span of a single day, they depleted the staff roster by half, poaching twenty four teachers from Aakash Institute, thirteen from the Janakpuri centre and eleven from South Extension. Jagdish the tiger roared in anger. He called an emergency meeting and in typical angry young man (Bachchan-style) asked the rest of the teaching staff to quit too. He declared that he could do the teaching all by himself. This was his way of shaking things up. The remaining teachers were loyalists and swore to stand by Chaudhry Sir.

He set a challenge for them, asking that they prove their loyalty by finding replacements for the teachers who had left. They would have to reach out to their friends and the teaching fraternity from Kanya Kumari to Kashmir. Their task was to help the Institute replace at least fourteen teachers by the next day.

He promised to escalate the salaries of the new hires by 50% if they got on a flight that night itself and reported to work at 10 am the next morning. To his pleasant surprise, eighteen excellent teachers were waiting for him in the office the next day.

Later on, when Aakash, a Harvard alumnus, joined the business, this kind of attrition rankled him. Aakash had moved to Mumbai where he formally took up a franchise from his father and ran it like a separate profit centre head. Four senior teachers quit on him unannounced one morning. Agitated, he called his father and asked him why they did not sign a bond with the teachers. Jagdish belonged to the old school of thought. He preferred to nurture loyalists and not be deterred by quitters. He instantly dispatched two of his trusted staff members to Mumbai overnight to turn the centre around. Subsequently, AESL went to make HR the cornerstone of its management policy, hiring a seasoned professional as Director to helm this operation.

Jagdish believes in creating a clear structure of reward-driven, periodic hikes. He has never bowed down to arm-twisting tactics and demands for out-of-turn salary hikes. Once, two teachers of Chemistry and Physics went incommunicado hours before their classes at the Ganesh Nagar centre. The duo could not be contacted over the phone. There was no trace of them, but Jagdish did not panic. He rushed to a baraat ghar (wedding merchandise shop) and rented some durries (rugs), which he spread out on the terrace of the Ganesh Nagar centre. Students from all the five sections were asked to come to the terrace which was lit up with makeshift bulbs.

Jagdish engaged the students by teaching Botany for three-and-a-half hours at a stretch. The terrace was full of spellbound students who felt privileged to be taught by Chaudhry Sir himself. They did not notice how the two teachers had been dexterously replaced. Jagdish held the classes for five days. On the sixth day, the errant teachers got back, mouthing some hard-to-believe excuses. Jagdish told them to collect their pending payments and leave. Matter closed, time to move on!

This initial experience taught him a valuable lesson. It helped him shape the teaching policy of Aakash Educational Services Ltd that is centred on a 'no star teacher policy'. Instead, the institution banks on the content and pedagogy developed by a sixty five-member National Academic Department. This content is delivered through well-trained faculty with the support of the finest technological tools in the industry.

Mantra 3: Loyalty is key and loyalists must be rewarded generously. Look after your trusted people as diligently as they have looked after you.

Trusted and faithful staff was always ready to bite the bullet for Chaudhry Sir. All his life, Jagdish has motivated and boosted his staff's morale, rewarding the faithful generously and standing by them in tough times.

A longtime employee, Kamleshwar Chawla shares, "I'll never forget how the Chaudhry family helped me in my darkest hour. In October 2003, I was informed at 11 one night that my husband who had gone to Manipal had suffered a massive heart attack. My son's final-year paper at AIIMS was slated for the next day. Shocked and shaken with grief, I called Chaudhry Sir. He immediately decided that his son, Dr. Aashish, would accompany me to Manipal. I requested that Dr. Aashish stay with me for the next three to four days till my husband stabilised. Sir assured me that Aashish was like my own son and I could rely on him."

Jagdish advises young startups to stand by their staff at all times. Encouraging and motivating the staff is paramount in his book. He never takes out the stress of running a huge coaching chain on the people he hires. Problems will crop up, but one has to have the resolve to handle them while motivating the staff with a smile every day. Failure is not a mark of shame. It is an opportunity to learn life lessons, a catalyst for improvement. Jagdish's signature move is to kill a negative with a positive and to never let his worries rub off on the staff.

Once, when the sealing drive in Delhi was at its peak, the staff at the Janakpuri centre was anxious about losing their jobs. "Sir called for an emergency meeting and we were convinced that he was going to announce the closure of the centre. Instead, he walked in, gave us a cheery pep talk, discussed the syllabus and left, says Dr. Surender Chauhan who heads the centres at Janakpuri, Raja Garden and Dwarka. Ritu Hajela remembers how Jagdish would readily step in when teachers missed their classes. He would even "drive all the way from South Extension to West Delhi within one hour to take on the role of substitute teacher for a class."

Jagdish also has the uncanny knack of spotting potential in the unlikeliest places. Rajesh Karna who was appointed as a peon at Aakash, and today runs the Aakash centres at Jammu and Udhampur, besides auditing the franchises at Srinagar. He was a quick and keen learner. Seeing this, Chaudhry Sir kept supporting his education and also gave him the job of maintaining the timetable at the Janakpuri centre. Karna's management skills were impressive and he slowly rose within the ranks.

Neelam Singh, a single parent, a skilled and efficient worker, was so absorbed in the job that she would often forget to pick up her son from school. When she said she wanted to run a hostel for Aakash's outstation students, Jagdish ensured her entrepreneurial dream became a reality. He has always encouraged promising employees to grow along with the organisation.

Mantra 4: Teaching is a dynamic profession that needs constant upgradation. Content is key.

Pure sciences are a dynamic field. Teachers need to keep up with all the changes that evolve based on ongoing research and development. They also have to keep realigning their course syllabi according to these upgrades.

Y.P. Purang, Executive Chairman, Delhi State Science Teacher's Forum and an old associate of Jagdish's shares, "In 1985, under the directive of the National Policy of Education, National Council of Educational Research and Training (NCERT) revised its curriculum. Biology saw the maximum changes with cell biology, genetics and bio-technology being added. The majority of Post-Graduate Teachers (PGTs) were not able to comprehend these changes. The forum organised seminars and training programmes for them. Jagdish came forward to help and soon became a very important resource in this close-knit group of educators. His USP was not only a deep understanding of genetics and cell biology, but also the ability to explain complex topics in a simple way."

When NCERT decided to include books published by individual publishers as per the new curriculum, Purang's publishers asked him to quickly write a book. Aware of Jagdish's expertise and his ability to adhere to deadlines, Purang invited him to co-author the book. Jagdish agreed and the book was completed in record time. It was included in the syllabi of Classes 9 and 12 and widely used.

Purang requested Jagdish to write an introductory book on Cell Biology and Genetics for teachers. Jagdish came up with a short, crisp book, listing all the FAQs pertaining to the subject. He answered them in his signature simple and straightforward style. His books became a trusted resource for both students and teacher. He has eight textbooks to his credit, many of them still in use by students of Classes 11 and 12.

Jagdish's group benefits immensely from this expertise of his. AESL creates content and methodology backed by solid research with continued investments in methods, delivery mechanisms and content to maintain the competitive edge of students.

Mantra 5: A business can be replicated, a brand cannot.

A young professional from a leading English daily taught Jagdish an unforgettable lesson early on. When asked to advertise the great results AESL was producing, Jagdish was reluctant. He did not want to throw away good money when word of mouth was working so well for AESL. Dominique's answer has stayed with him. He said that in the absence of a brand anyone could replicate Aakash's business.

All they needed was a crore as capital and office space. However, no one could take the place of an established and well-recognised brand. This made a deep impact on him and Jagdish started placing full-page advertisements in national dailies regularly from then on. The number of pages went up soon as Aakash Institute decided to feature every student who had gained admission, not just the rank holders. This move, he says, also helped transition the hitherto unorganised industry of coaching into a brand-driven and organised sector.

Mantra 6: People pay happily for quality.

For the first few years, AESL kept the fees highly subsidised. The founder wanted to help shape and influence the lives of young professionals and change young people's fates for good. The students and their parents showered praises on the management for this. There was much goodwill. Parents would come by to the centres with boxes of sweets to thank Jagdish and the staff. However, this only lasted for the first few years. The number of thankful parents visiting the centres dwindled. Some even started joking that Aakash should be paying them for piggybacking on the fame of their children's success and using it to build its brand.

Jagdish realised that missionary zeal was not enough. He shifted gears and took into account the bottom line: driven by money. He hiked the fees since he believed that people would pay for quality. How he transitioned to an 80% fee hike in three weeks is quite a tale! Week one, he raised the fees by 30% and printed new brochures. No one batted an eyelid. The next Monday, he raised it again by 20%, printed new flyers and tore up the previous ones. Again, there was no reaction. Within a week he had torn up brochure number two as well and raised the fees by 30%. He immediately circulated a note to all the enrolled students that if they did not agree with the fee hike, they were welcome to get a refund. Only two parents responded. The rest were willing to spend what it took to help their children soar to the sky.

From 2008 onwards, the consolidation and rapid growth phase of AESL began. The founder though never forgot the early phase of strife and the lessons he had learnt about turning negative actions into positive reactions. The angry young Bachchan was now ready to turn into a calm Dilip Kumar and he handed over the baton to his son, Aakash Chaudhry, allowing him to charge ahead with full enthusiasm and ensuring him that his father was always available to advise, if needed. Jagdish stopped teaching his subject, Botany, from 2008. Till 2018, he travelled from city to city across India to motivate students, teachers and parents, gradually converting his coaching institutes into a legendry organisation based on ethical values.

8

Taking The Legacy Forward

Inheritance is a tricky matter for both the founder of an enterprise and the ones stepping into the founder's shoes. Every business house, big or small, arrives at this milestone at some point. The founder must make space for the younger generation and fresh ideas. The inheritors have to remember what a great responsibility is being placed on their shoulders and also be grateful for the empire they inherit. As Warren Buffet aptly puts it, "someone sitting in the shade must not forget that someone planted the tree long ago."

Jagdish had planted the seeds and tended to them, dedicating the prime of his life to nurturing the tree of life. Aakash Institute was the result of his relentless hard work and persistence. So far, his son Aakash had lived a relatively carefree life. But now, it was time for him to pitch in and learn everything that he needed to know about managing the institution, protecting it and leading it to greater heights.

This transition process was daunting and had to be handled cautiously. Both Aashish and Aakash were brought up to be intelligent, independent and dynamic people with minds of their own. Both were driven by their individual passions to carve out their own space under the sun. Both also knew that the education empire their father had built needed a family member to take it forward. Aashish, the elder son, by choosing to be a doctor, had started to charter his own path. Aakash, on the other hand, was aware that he had the option to tend to his aspirations under the shade of the tree his father had so painstakingly grown.

The Chaudhrys had worked hard to make sterling people out of their young sons. Resilient, high on values, hard working and honest—the boys had grown into fine men. The couple had prepared their sons for life's ups and down. Their upbringing was rooted in certain principles that are guaranteed to make leaders out of people. Self-reliance was an all important principle. Aashish and Aakash had been left to fend for themselves more than once in their young lives. Their parents let them experience real-life jolts to toughen them up.

The Chaudhrys were strict disciplinarians, but they followed the carrot and stick policy. The toughness was always laced with love. Jagdish was the unrelenting disciplinarian and Kamla, the friend, comrade-in-arms and confidante. She was the hands-on parent, listening to the boys' stories, breaking up their fights, satisfying their every whim when they were children. She also kept a meticulous study roster for their father to review. "She was his spy who reported our every academic move and miss to him," Aashish laughs.

Aakash considers his mother a close friend. He feels free to play childish pranks on her and joke with her. He shares his hopes and dreams—even the impossible ones—with her. With his father, however, he has always drawn clear boundaries. "My mother instilled the right values in me and I inherited my business acumen from my father," he says.

All through their growing-up years, Jagdish resolutely took the high road with his sons. Hearing him talk about it, one is reminded of another Warren Buffet quote, "I'll give my children enough money so that they would feel they could do anything, but not so much that they could do nothing." For this father, however, the rationing of resources did not stop at money. He was a big leveller—he rationed the privileges of both Aashish and Aakash. This stemmed from the principal that children should not bask in the glory of their father, a self-made man. Instead they had to make their own mark on the world. Jagdish was determined to instill in his sons a value for money and a keen sense of profit and loss. He spoke of enterprise with his sons and drilled it into their heads that even if they used the resources of Aakash Institute, they had to become profit centre heads and ensure returns for every business they set up. Hence, when Aashish took up a family-owned space to run his orthopedic clinic later on, Jagdish clearly told him about the returns that were expected from him. When Aakash headed the franchise of Aakash Institute at Mumbai, he had to share 25% of the revenue with him as a license fee.

Both boys followed a substantial academic path to their careers. Aashish fulfilled his father's dream of becoming a doctor and Aakash decided to choose engineering. Jagdish had always hoped to see one of his sons become a doctor, which he admits was a matter of living vicariously. As a young man, he had dreamt of becoming a doctor himself and later on, he had seen so many young students joining the profession. He yearned for his eldest son to don a doctor's white coat and nudged Aashish in that direction. Aashish had become fascinated by the profession after hearing his father talk about all the students who had cracked the entrance exams and gained admission at medical colleges. Hoping to join their ranks, he did the obvious. When he was in Class 11, he enrolled at the nearest Aakash Institute. As Chaudhry Sir's son he simply had to succeed. Good results must begin at home, his father always said. This was a make or break moment for both his father and for Aakash Institute.

There were no concessions for Aashish, no special privileges, no extra classes, no special notes or individual tutorials by the legend. Instead he was asked to source the notes by himself if he missed classes and made to sit on the bench outside if he walked in late. His father did not reserve any special time for him. Instead, he had to face a volley of tough questions in class and he felt humiliated when was unable to answer some of them. Aashish was under a lot of pressure. He felt that if he did not get admission at a reputed medical college, his father's twenty years of hard work would amount to nothing. Young Aashish was also perturbed because his father was being extra tough on him. Jagdish had his reasons. He was putting Aashish through the grind because he wanted to inspire his son to be the best possible version of himself. The tiger was coaching his cub to go for the kill.

After he appeared for AIPMT, he saw his father lower his guard and celebrate for the first time. Aashish remembers the day of the test clearly. When he came home from the examination centre, he saw his father enjoying his Sunday ritual of pouring himself a glass of beer, tucking into the great meal cooked by Kamla and then taking a power nap. When woke up, he sat down with Aashish and dissected his test paper threadbare. When he was satisfied by his son's answers and was fully confident that he would ace the exam, he offered him a glass of beer! Aashish calls this his first icebreaker with his strict father.

Aashish did his father and the Institute proud by acing the major exams including the Delhi Pre-Medical Test in which he ranked 20, Armed Forces Medical College (AFMC), Aligarh Muslim University (AMU) and JIPMER. Spoilt for choice, he eventually enrolled at Maulana Azad Medical College (MAMC), where he completed the first leg of a long drawn-out educational process.

Though Jagdish believed in tough love, both his sons never grudged him his toughness. In fact, they could see past his stern demeanour easily. Tough on the outside, he was essentially a soft-hearted man, a loving father who promised to stand by their side through thick and thin. If they were in trouble, he would come to their rescue at once. He was the rock on which they could always lean on.

Aashish understood this clearly after he completed his MBBS in 2001. At this time, he faced many a tough situation in his life. He was determined to take up surgery as his specialty and study in the United States. He cleared the United States Medical Licensing Exam (USMLE). However, a visa issue destroyed his dream.

He had to change his plans and seek admission in a UK-based college. He wanted to practice in the UK and for this; he had to appear for PLAB, a written exam consisting of multiple choice questions. This attempt did not succeed. Eventually, he majored in orthopedic surgery from Lady Harding Medical College, Delhi. The setbacks he had faced despite ranking 20 in the Delhi PMT and qualifying for many other colleges, bogged him down. Throughout this turbulent period, he found a staunch ally in his father. Jagdish was his sounding board, support system and punching bag. He trusted his father implicitly.

Aakash also recalls an incident when he committed a big mistake while apprenticing at Aakash Institute. Unable to sort out the mess, he eventually gathered the courage to walk up to his father's room. One look at Aakash's ashen face and Jagdish knew something was terribly wrong. He gave his son a patient hearing and told him to forget about it, assuring him that the whole thing was now his problem.

~

Aakash first joined the business fresh out of engineering college in 2001. That was the year of an economic meltdown, the bubble had burst and he lost his job at Tata Consultancy Services. His stint with the family business lasted for a very short time though. When most family-run businesses ask their heirs to come work at the office, they are expected to be of silent observers who absorb the work culture. The heir is possibly placed in the most innocuous of positions. He is part of the system, but the founder is very much the figure at the top at this point. While this might have worked with mediocre minds, Aakash was restless and full of plans for change that he wanted to incorporate. On hindsight, he admits that many of his proposed ideas were a tad immature and quickly disposed of by his father. The young, hot-blooded Aakash informed his father that they were "very different people and could never work together."

Thereafter, he moved on to charter a path in the tech business. To begin with, he pursued a short-term management course at National University of Singapore (NUS). Soon after that, he decided to pursue an MBA and joined ISB, Hyderabad. He also completed the Owner President Management (OPM) Course at Harvard Business School. Then came a stint with leading tech companies like Infosys and Cognizant. By studying management theory and working with global giants and tech MNCs, Aakash's random thoughts were replaced by targeted and result-eliciting theories of growth and sustenance. His father was thrilled by this evolution.

In 2006, Aakash was "lovingly conned" into joining the family business as he often jokes. While working for Cognizant at Chennai, he was living the typical young techie life: five working days, Friday nights at the pub, weekend excursions to Pondicherry and Bengaluru. He was all set to tie the knot with Neetu who was active in the world of design and lived in Mumbai. Since she was not enthusiastic about living in Chennai, Aakash had sought a four-year assignment to Australia. The two of them were planning to move there soon after the wedding.

His parents hated the idea. Their heir was running away from the country and they did not know what to do. A family panchayat was called and all the elders huddled together. Jagdish sought advice from his elder brother Jai Dayal who had just returned after a long teaching stint in the United States. All of them agreed that they could not let Aakash leave, no matter how much he insisted.

During one of his visits home from Chennai, the family ambushed Aakash. His parents and Uncle Jai Dayal sat him down and read him the riot act. Jagdish insisted that he needed a family member to help him run his business. Otherwise all his hard work over the years would be in vain. Uncle Jai said he too was willing to chip in and help, now that he was retired and had more time on his hands. His mother became very emotional. Aakash insisted that he needed to feel free to be his own person if he joined the family business. He wanted to find his own groove and apply the management theories of growth he had imbibed. Jagdish agreed to all his demands at once.

Kamla remembers, "As parents, my husband and I never wanted to cramp our sons' space or force them to do things they did not enjoy. At the same time, we both hoped that Aakash would stand shoulder to shoulder with his father and turn into his main support. Aashish as a surgeon had his life's course chartered for him. In Aakash, we sensed the business acumen to be his father's second-in-command."

The ice melted, a consensus was reached, the battle won. However, Aakash was clear that if he stuck close to Jagdish, his father would protect him and not allow him to make any mistakes and learn from them. The family panchayat decided to send Aakash to Mumbai to flag off a franchise there. It would be treated as a real franchise and would involve the payment of royalty to the head office. Aakash agreed to this and went back to Chennai to submit his resignation, citing his marriage as the excuse. The techie was forgotten, the educationist born.

In his earlier stint at the South Extension Institute as a counsellor Aakash had been exposed to the sentiments and aspirations of both students and parents. It was this awareness that was his biggest inspiration as he moved to Mumbai, which was a new market for Aakash Institute. The region offered strong competition for the Institute. Besides, the Maharashtra state level entrance exam, Combined Entrance Test (CET), was not mapped out for CBSE. Instead it followed the Maharashtra Board exam syllabus. All the notes prepared by Aakash Institute were custom-made for CBSE.

The market and the exam format were new for Aakash's brand which held sway over North India. Aakash had a big job on hand. Along with scouting for office space, interviewing teachers and staff, he had to also oversee the creation of fresh notes and content that was mapped out for CET and the Maharashtra Board syllabus.

Opening a franchise turned out to be the best way to initiate Aakash into the business. As a franchisee, he was literally running the show, right from opening the centre at 7 a.m., to managing the teachers and the non-teaching staff. He woke up every Saturday at the crack of dawn to ensure his pamphlets were placed in all the newspapers. He scoped out the competition and became an expert at handling tough situations. He was so caught up in this role that after getting married in November 2005, he was back at work by the end of December 2005 itself. He settled down into the driver's seat of Aakash Institute's first franchise at Mumbai's Andheri East, becoming Jagdish's trusted general. The franchise was successfully flagged off on 13 March, 2006.

Interestingly, his parents had sent along a family member to Mumbai to keep a close watch on Aakash and be his support system. Jagdish's big brother Jai Dayal decided to open a franchise in Pune. Nephew and uncle, living in the same geographical zone, became each other's support system, comparing notes every evening and cheering each other on through tough days.

The franchise Aakash headed ran into some hurdles at the start. Within the first week of beginning operations, two teachers left without giving notice and handing in their resignations. Aakash was shocked. He called up his father and confronted him. Why were teachers, the most valuable of resources, not made to sign a bond or be held accountable in some way? Jagdish, a veteran at this, told his angry son that he was lucky to face this roadblock so soon in his career trajectory. He advised Aakash to combine classes and ask teachers to take double the number of classes. He also sent two trusted teachers by air to replace the resources they had lost. Aakash received them at the airport, acutely aware of the importance of teaching staff in an educational enterprise. They were three months away from the entrance test and everything was new: the city, the staff, the syllabus and the notes. What was old and trusted was the confidence that their attempt would succeed. And it did!

Eight of the eleven Aakashians who appeared for CET got through and Aakash Chaudhry was over the moon. Parents and students showered him with thanks and praise. They were grateful to him for opening the Institute in Mumbai and saving them the bother of going all the way to Delhi to enroll there. He recalls teasing his father that his score of eight out of eleven was better than Delhi's score of seven out of twelve. A proud Aakash assured his father, "Now I will handle it all."

He had found a way to combine his innovative ideas with the wealth of his father's experience and vision to flag off a long, eventful journey of change, disruption and innovation. He was the organisation's changemaker, and together, Jagdish and he made a perfect team. Though well established, the organisation was still not a large one when Aakash joined it in 2006. Aakash Institute was clocking a turnover of 8–9 crore a year and had self-run centres in Delhi and Dehradun as well as a few franchises. Through innovative formats, the group was also catering to feeder markets.

Chaudhry Sir, a teacher at heart, was focusing on the core deliverables expected of an institute. He was running the centres hands on, handling the teachers, and preparing the students for the exams. Everything revolved around Jagdish, the teacher with the Midas touch and there was a linear management team to supplement his drive. In any case the scale of the business did not demand a layered hierarchy. Nor was Jagdish willing to get into frenzied expansion mode at the cost of quality. The next growth curve, the brand disruption and expansion happened shortly after Aakash entered the fray.

9

The Changemaker

When Aakash grew comfortable with the role of the franchisee of Aakash Institute, Mumbai, he made his father a very happy man. Jagdish was proud of the fact that his son was complimenting his leadership goals. Aakash had put Aakash Institute on the map of Maharashtra, with sterling support from his uncle Jai Dayal, the backbone of the Pune centre. He was beginning to take an active interest in the business and looking at it with a fresh perspective. Aakash's involvement gave a new sense of hope to his father. In Aakash, Jagdish saw the bright future of his education empire. Aakash was the one person who would care for what he had built—with the same intensity, sincerity and dedication as him.

Aakash's progress reassured Jagdish that his son did not regret missing the chance to live the life of a techie in distant Australia. Jagdish was deeply conscious of having held Aakash back from moving to Australia. He wanted to do everything to make sure that the decision benefitted his son. With this thought in mind, he gave a great deal of freedom to Akash to mould Aakash Institute, now AESL (incorporated in 2006), according to his vision. When Aakash had set the functioning of the Mumbai centre on auto pilot, he returned to Delhi, all geared up to work at the corporate office. The stint in Mumbai had taught him all about the nitty gritty of the business, its highs and lows.

The Shishya was now fully aware of how the Guru had created the blue print of the enterprise and how the business had evolved over the years. He had realised that Aakash Institute's management edifice worked on the foundation of the instincts and clear vision of the founder. Jagdish was well assisted, of course, by his battery of trusted employees and close confidantes. Many of them had humble beginnings just like Jagdish. All his hardworking and sincere teammates were like family, sharing a one-on-one equation with him.

Once he came back to the head office, Aakash felt the need to grow the business both geographically and exponentially. Growth, for any thriving business, is inevitable. How much, how healthy and how organised is what makes all the difference. Large multi-national organisations have clear SOPs, carefully chartered growth plans, precisely dotted milestones and enough capital to tide them through thick and thin. Individually driven, organic and personalised businesses like AESL tend to grow in all directions, often making the model lop-sided and a bit skewed. Just like a tree grows in whichever direction the sun commands it to, organisations that are helmed by a singular visionary often tend to follow his light, moulding themselves according to his singular vision.

Aakash Institute in the mid-2000s was a perfect example of this. It was growing in tune to the abilities of the man at the top. Jagdish was a self-made entrepreneur, result driven and focused, but first and foremost a teacher. The fine nuances of management theories, or "jargon", as he likes to call it, was not on his list of priorities. For him, the process of cause and effect was simple—if there is a crisis, solve it; if there is achievement, reward it; if there are good results, share them with the world and if things go awry with any staffers, bid them a decent farewell.

Jagdish, an educator at the core, gave most of his time to what he felt were the core deliverables of a coaching institute. He devoted his energy to crafting a well-syllabus, motivating students to succeed by inspiring them with his charisma as well as his in depth knowledge, ensuring teachers helped students to revise their subjects in the minutest detail, and watching them like a hawk as they appeared for mock tests.

For him, growth was always opportunity and need based. With his supremely intuitive instincts, he could sense potential in a region. An opportunity arose when a promising franchisee approached him to open a centre on a piece of land with his capital.

This franchisee plan as formulated by Jagdish was straightforward and linear like all the earlier business formats created by him. Every quid pro quo was clearly defined and listed with scientific precision. For a coaching institute, the franchisee model had to focus on ensuring a high percentage of toppers and large numbers of admissions to various medical colleges. This was not just the end goal but also the profit multiplier. Hence, the franchiser lent his entire expertise in structuring, monitoring, and executing the course syllabus, study material, pedagogy guidelines, etc., to the franchisee and also tweaked them from time to time. The franchiser was also deeply involved in the selection of teachers, each one personally hired, trained and monitored by a group of seasoned educators who had worked with the Institute for over a decade. They were experts in the business of coaching. This group comprised of the brand custodians of the organisation and their job was to travel from franchise to franchise, training, strengthening and assisting the teaching staff there.

The franchisee had certain obligations. Their responsibility was to provide the space, the capital to meet all expenses and the marketing prowess to succeed. Fees, which were structured and standardised, were collected by the franchisee, with Aakash asking for its royalty at the end of the month. With his roots and acclaim firmly tied to Delhi, the capital city, Jagdish was clear on one point: Aakash Institute would only have centres driven by the head office in Delhi. All franchisee arrangements would be made in places outside the city. The Group had seven corporate-driven institutes, six in Delhi and one in Dehradun, along with twenty two franchised branches spread across north and west India. To a management graduate like Aakash, this ratio looked a bit skewed, given the lack of control one eventually had on a franchisee.

Having set up the Mumbai centre personally, and now running it effectively from Delhi, he realised that they could set up as many centres as they wanted. He was convinced that franchisee arrangements had the potential of being any quality-driven business's nemesis. These could easily be done away with and replaced with centres which consulted closely with the head office and run by staff appointed and monitored by the Group. "Why give out franchises?" was Aakash's mantra for change. Instead, he recruited able managers to run the branches across the country. Many of them were long time, trusted employees who had a keen grasp of the company's work style and corporate philosophy. All he needed to do was place them in a position of authority and accountability. He had created very clear work guidelines and standard operating procedures for the branch in Pune and Mumbai. It was not difficult to replicate them over and over again.

Standardisation, organisation, innovation and replication were the four pillars on which Aakash based his vision of remodelling AESL. He skillfully combined his father's experience and knowledge with his expertise in logic and data. His stint in the world outside of AESL had taught him one crucial lesson: the only way to grow was with a vision backed by clear-cut growth plans. He was well exposed to the various management principles he had learnt during his stint in ISB. While pursuing the OPM programme at Harvard, he had met many contemporaries who had helped their inherited companies to transition to well-oiled organisations. Their stories of daring paradigm shifts with reference to self-made enterprises spurred him on.

The roles were redefined this time: Aakash proposed, Jagdish met the idea with skepticism, Aakash then backed his proposal with scientific data, Jagdish happily gave in. To build a parallel to the series of conversations between father and son during this period, it is apt to refer to the Bhagvad Gita and explore the many verbal exchanges between Lord Krishna and Arjuna the famed archer. Just like Arjuna questioned every war plan based on his experience, Jagdish needed convincing in adapting to a more structured and orderly war plan formulated by Aakash. A shift towards standardisation was not easy for a leader who followed his instincts and had thus far built most relationships at the workplace on humane and personal grounds.

The first step Aakash took was to standardise operations and create clear SOPs that would help in the multiplier process. He hired Ernst & Young to create clear playbooks for every work arena and the staff responsible for it. No one was spared: the counsellor, the cashier, the accountant, the branch manager and the teacher now had a ready operation manual to refer to. This manual came into play every time a new employee was brought on board. Jagdish was skeptical. He wanted to know why employees should be restricted to a fixed mould. Why should the Institute use important resources to train those who were already skilled and qualified to do their jobs?

Aakash argued that this was the best way to ensure that every person they employed was properly initiated into the organisation's work ethic. They would report to work aware of all the rules, leaving little room for mistakes, and hence saving the management precious time, energy and money. A firm believer in the adage that good teachers are born, not made, Jagdish was doubtful about training them. If a teacher had the aptitude, students were bound to listen and learn. Aakash had an answer to that: an untrained teaching resource would simply waste both the student's and the Institute's time. If the Institute allowed every teacher to adopt his or her own teaching style, the process would be chaotic. Many teachers would have to be fired and the Institute would acquire the reputation of being unable to retain their staff. Jagdish was convinced. From then on, he personally oversaw the training programme and ensured every teacher became familiar with the work ethos of AESL.

"No one questioned the decision because it came from Chairman Sir," says a proud Aakash. This was a ploy he employed every time he wanted to introduce something new. "Once I convinced him about something, he was like a child," Aakash says about his father. "He would be eager to implement the change and ensure it was done in a thorough manner."

~

In 2007, Aakash Institute went ahead and added an IIT-JEE programme for engineering aspirants to its list. A student of engineering himself,

Aakash saw great merit in coaching students in this equally sought after stream. "In smaller towns, the only two relevant careers were that of doctor and engineer. It was important for us to address both these streams," he recalls. Aakash IIT-JEE was born to provide test preparatory services for engineering aspirants. Within a few years, the programme could boast about producing a Rank One in IIT and Aakash's happiness knew no bounds. He was especially thrilled when Jagdish gave him the backhanded compliment that the son had got a Rank One much faster than the father who was the teacher! Despite the many difficulties he had faced in life, Jagdish kept his childlike enthusiasm alive. Aakash, as well as the entire rank and file of AESL, found this trait of their Chairman Sir inspirational.

To grow in the business of education, the most important asset one needs is teachers. If AESL wanted to play the numbers game they needed to overcome their biggest roadblock—not having a steady supply of teachers. Pondering about this endlessly, Aakash hit upon a solution in 2009. He proposed that they attend the various IIT campus placement programmes to hire engineering graduates as teachers for the Aakash centres that were mushrooming across India. To begin with, Jagdish found it an overtly ambitious and impossible dream.

His son thought otherwise and convinced him, once again, with the help of logic and statistics. Aakash had it all worked out: he was going to reach out to students in the lesser-known IIT centres in India. He would also approach BTech students from other non-IIT colleges as well as graduates in pure science from reputed institutes. He was not going to reach out to tech graduates or mechanical engineers who were sought after by global MNCs. Instead, he got in touch with graduates in material science, textile engineering and other courses and offered them pay packages that were at par with market rates.

His logic was very simple: these were students who had cracked the IIT entrance test and knew the test-prep game first hand. They were above average in academics. Many came from humble backgrounds had already given Maths and Science tuitions to students, even while they were studying in order to supplement the meager funds provided by their parents. Hence teaching was not an alien process for them. And above all, they were young, enthusiastic, and just about three or four years older than the students and able to strike up an easy camaraderie with them.

Aakash left no stone unturned. He prepared a fantastic pre-placement presentation that detailed the fast-paced growth trajectory envisioned by the group; the joy young graduates felt working at Aakash, the sense of gratification one experiences for having changed someone's life for the better. Such was the enthusiasm he drummed up that in the first year itself they were able to hire 250 IITians as Aakash Institute teachers. Interestingly, while the graduates needed little convincing, their parents had to be assured that this was a prestigious job. Many were reluctant initially because they had not scrounged up every penny to see their children turning into science teachers at a coaching centre after graduating from IIT.

Aakash managed to win them over. The IITians he hired to teach were inducted into Aakash's style of pedagogy by the seasoned and trusted staff of the Institute. Some of the old timers were shaken by the brood of youngsters who had stormed their bastion. They went complaining to their beloved Chaudhry Sir who in turn quizzed his son about the value of this decision. Aakash put forth his case very strongly. His contention was that these teachers were young, go-getters and brimming with fresh ideas. Their attendance record was impeccable. They were bringing out the best in the students, striking up an excellent rapport with them and making themselves available to the students day and night. The results they produced were ample proof as were the rave reviews from parents. Their enthusiasm made up for their limited work experience. Jagdish was convinced by this argument and Aakash's battle was won.

The management now had firepower: an army of teachers to walk the talk. Bold steps became the norm and many new centres were set up. Jagdish knew the pulse of the business. He could pinpoint the regions in the country that were high yielding in terms of consumers of the test prep format. Southern India for instance was a big market since it was teeming with aspirants. Jagdish decided to open twenty centres in the region one after the other. Today, there are 214 AESL brick and mortar centres in the country. 145 of these are run by the management and 69 given to franchisees, which are regularly audited by the corporate team.

Jagdish felt that the many aspirants who made a beeline for the Delhi centres would stop enrolling there and so he initially viewed the foray into markets outside Delhi with skepticism. His fear was that if the branches outside Delhi did well, no one would care about Delhi. And if they did not do well, that would create a dent in the excellent reputation of the brand. Despite Jagdish's apprehensions, father and son agreed that Delhi would remain their focus and they would go ahead and open a number of centres outside the city as well. This did not work out well at the start. Parents who were in awe of the results produced by Delhi easily bypassed the Aakash Institute branches in their towns and packed off their children to Delhi. The centres in Delhi had to deal with more demand than supply while branches elsewhere were not filled to capacity.

Realising he had to correct this imbalance, Jagdish decided to charge up every branch with his inimitable pedagogy. He personally travelled from city to city, motivating the students, training the teachers and tweaking the courses till commendable results started pouring in. The icing on the cake was that the enrollment at the Delhi centres held steady and the numbers at the branches hit the roof. Both Jagdish and Aakash were delighted by this development. Their hard work had produced the required turnaround.

The camaraderie father and son share is near perfect. One speaks, the other executes; two minds in sync with each other. While Aakash calls himself his father's foot soldier, Jagdish listens patiently to all his son's ideas. Nothing is dismissed without a hearing, however far-fetched and revolutionary it may sound to begin with. Once, Aakash insisted on convening a parent teacher meeting. Jagdish thought this would be murder! Parents would descend on them with their sky-high ambitions and eat them alive. He told his son to not step into the tiger's den. Even the staff at the Institute was convinced that this was a bad idea. Aakash, however, was clear that he wanted to get the parents' perspective. After all, they were a significant part of the business and their voices could not be ignored or their views pushed under the carpet.

The meeting was set up. It began on a volatile note; parents were eager to voice their pent-up opinions and clamouring to be heard. They screamed and vented. Aakash heard them out quietly, jotting down points, telling them how he valued their viewpoints. By the end of the meeting, he had compiled eighty relevant suggestions, many of which were revelations of sorts. Aakash shared these points with his father. This was what the parents wanted and no one had brought it to Jagdish's notice so far. Jagdish was grateful to his son for this exercise. He was so impressed that he ordered all centres to conduct a parent-teacher meeting and make it a biannual feature from then on.

Aakash, the pampered younger son, had come into his own. Now in the driver's seat, he was truly value adding to the group. Slowly, Jagdish started to place his trust in Aakash and give him a free hand. "He just needed convincing and once he was convinced then there was no looking back," says a grateful Aakash. The two were best friends now and his stern father was someone he could be completely at ease with.

"He was always so busy," Aakash recalls. "When we were kids we only saw him rush in and out of the house. Right until 1993, we did not even know that he was running an institute called Aakash. Aashish and I thought he was a teacher. That's it...I remember he treated us to ice cream when twenty three of his students got into AIPMT in 1993. He kept talking about the results while I was only interested in the ice cream."

~

The two pillars of standardisation were achieved but organisation and innovation remained to be addressed. While the latter is an ongoing process and has led to many firsts, the former was yet another target Aakash successfully met. Having grown organically, AESL did not have hierarchies and talents to fit each rung. For instance there was a single HR manager, the finance was handled by an accountant and the tech department was the responsibility of a data operator. Aakash, ably assisted by his father, built an entirely new infrastructure, sourcing, interviewing and hiring the best talent pool to lead the growth plan. For this, he relied on his father whose instincts about people were laser sharp. Jagdish was not just instinctive about people; he could also assess their past and future using his expertise in the science of numerology.

He is a celebrated numerologist, with a channel to which millions subscribe. Jagdish used his grasp of numerology to assess the character of a person and also to gauge their compatibility with his organisation. Once the whole pool of professionals was in place, the group started creating a second version of SOPs, clearly defining the deliverables, key role areas and accountability checks and balances.

Each year a fresh crop of centres was added to the repertoire. It was a steady growth curve, carefully nurtured and monitored by Aakash. Having evolved into an educator, Aakash had begun to dream of opening a school. Jagdish, the visionary, felt that schools should follow a not-for-profit business model and anything that did not yield a monetary return was an indulgence that they could not afford at a time when the group was still growing in increments. So, every time there was talk of opening a school, Aakash was packed off to open ten new centres across the country.

Though his school plan was put on hold, the need to value add to the learning process at the school level was something Aakash was committed to. This lead to the birth of the Foundation Course at Aakash Institute—one of the many positive disruptions introduced by Aakash.

Today, the Institute provides comprehensive test-prep services to students from Classes 11 and 12, preparing them for the medical and engineering entrance examinations, and Foundation Courses to students from Classes 8 to 10. It also provides several foundation level scholarship exams and Olympiads, classroom based coaching services and digital and distance learning, which supplement the classroom courses and allow students to engage in independently-paced learning.

AESL, founded and consolidated by Jagdish, flourished under the joint leadership of father and son.

10

Ed To Ed Tech

There is an ominous threat every second-generation family-run business faces: that of becoming obsolete in practices and getting caught up in the vicious cycle of reinvesting one's own capital over and over again till young, tech-led and edgy brands with fresh practices and investors take over. The generation gap between founders and their inheritors, a dogged refusal by the founder to change and adapt to the times and ego clashes amongst the next generation tears many family businesses apart. Jagdish calls this simply a lack of vision on the part of the founder and a sense of proprietary on the part of his/her children who feel it is their birthright to step into a readymade empire and call the shots.

His mantra is that time and thoughts must run parallel and what holds true today should not be the gospel tomorrow. In fact, he endorses the fact that change is the only constant and believes that if a business has to go on then the scions need to be more involved in it than the founder and take on challenges, feel the adrenaline pumping through their systems and have the same drive that he himself felt each day when he sat in the driver's seat. The eagerness to take the business forward is a crucial ingredient for the success of the second-generation leadership.

To Jagdish, the fact that his younger son, Aakash, entered the education business and wholeheartedly devoted himself to it was a gift from Maa Vaishno Devi, his beloved Goddess who lives in the mountains. Once Aakash stepped into the driver's seat, Jagdish stepped back and took to the navigator's seat. Much like Lord Krishna guided Arjuna's chariot, Jagdish wisely supplemented his son's every move. And sure enough, the core team shunned obsolete practices, making innovation and progress centrifugal to their growth.

By 2013, AESL had proliferated across the country with centres mushrooming in every city and town. Not only was AESL opening several new centres but also turning into the market leader with a growth rate that was steady, quality driven and result oriented. More and more centres saw students making it to the merit list of reputed professional colleges and going on to become great successes in their chosen fields. This was the right time for AESL to focus on innovation and new mediums of coaching that would open up new geographical markets. More importantly, the group felt the urgent need to embrace technology and reach out to more students through innovative educational offerings.

With the rise in urbanisation, India's average annual urban population growth rate doubled and AESL's need to innovate coincided with the growth of the Indian middle class. As larger numbers of Indians became educated and built a steady lifestyle, they wanted to grow, move forward and become more affluent. Families saw education as the only way forward for their children. Millions of middle-class families aspired to see their daughters and sons become doctors and engineers, especially in smaller towns where there was lesser exposure to alternative career options. They realigned their children's entire education with this singular goal in mind. To get their children admitted to a premier medical or engineering college became their lives' raison d'être. A child's orientation started as early as when they were in Class 8 and the entire family's life circled around providing them the best possible coaching for the entrance exams that would they have to appear for after completing their schooling.

With this level of commitment by so many families, the test-prep market was set to explode. India, with thirty two million enrollments in higher education in 2013, was ranked second in the world, after

China, which had thirty four million enrollments. India has the highest number of higher education institutions at around 52,599 as per the All India Survey on Higher Education's provisional report of 2015–2016. As the demand for test-prep institutes increased, so did the geographical scope of its outreach.

The advent of technology and the ease of communication it offered made the test-prep market more accessible to larger segments of student. The trick was to innovate for change and embrace this new world inhabited by a generation of youngsters who had an inbuilt affinity for computers and technology.

Aakash says, "There was a sudden surge of awareness about career advancement through success in entrance exams and a larger number of families were factoring in this aspect to their children's education. Besides, when we entered the smaller cities we realised that there was so much talent, so many intelligent and capable children who could not be reached through the brick and mortar format alone. Also, as entrance exams got tougher and the number of students appearing for these exams grew, good results by test-prep players became linked to the ability to scout the highest calibre students in your cadre. They had to be highly intelligent but also young enough to be moulded into geniuses. The other crucial factor was that technological advancements in communication became more accessible to the remotest regions of India at this time."

Add to this Jagdish's inherent need to give back to the world the abundance it had bestowed on him. He believed that truly talented children, especially those from financially challenged backgrounds, must be supported and given a fair chance to find a place in the professional world. "I knew first hand the Himalayan route you had to take to reach a professional college. This is especially true for students who attended remote village schools in the early years of their lives, and spent their time with other children who had little motivation to excel." Determined to help the many J.C. Chaudhrys in the making, AESL set up scholarship schemes for such students.

After mapping out emerging trends with precision, AESL laid out a three-pronged growth programme that focused on three key words:

technology, calibre and starting them young. With these words in mind, the father-son team of AESL charted yet other pioneering path for the test-prep market. Embracing technology wholeheartedly, AESL decided to create a format for taking their lecture modules online. In order to find students with the potential to excel and the grit to win against all odds, AESL introduced a series of scholarship programmes based on the results of a set of competitive exams, which have become the benchmark for excellence today. Starting them young was a must and hence AESL's Foundation Programme, introduced in 2009, was strengthened and given as much presence and teeth as the divisions that handled the test-prep for AIPMT and JEE.

There were little or no facilities in terms of technology in smaller towns for training students to ace the competitive exams. AESL saw this as a major opportunity to expand their geographical reach within the country. The main setback to this growth of online education was connectivity, especially in rural areas. But, between 2014 and 2018, data usage per subscriber increased fifteen times. The sheer convenience of sourcing the course material at home, the cost factor that made online coaching courses highly affordable, and the ease of being able to refer to digitised lectures umpteen times made Aakash's digital courses veritable stars in tier-two and tier-three towns.

Initially, Jagdish had slight reservations about making Aakash Institute's tutorials and lectures freely available online. His question was that if students could access the classes in the comfort of their homes, then why would they bother to trudge to a brick-and-mortar class ever again. Aakash convinced his father otherwise, asking him to give the digitised lectures, which he believed would add sheen to Jagdish's legendary image and also help to take the brand forward. Aakash argued that since Jagdish was the true synonym of the brand, any medical or engineering aspirant attending his extremely engaging classes online would feel the burning desire to explore more and seek Aakash's educational offerings. In sync with the technology in vogue at the time, these lectures were recorded and CD-ROMs were created, patented and sold under the AESL banner. They were widely distributed especially in southern India where education is a top priority for people.

The online lectures were a huge success. J.C. Chaudhry, the teacher with the Midas touch, became a household name. As a result, aspirants from both rural and urban India, nurturing a deep desire to enroll at a coaching college, started to search for the nearest Aakash Institute while banking on the CD-ROMs for basic guidance. The lectures by Chaudhry Sir set the ball rolling. As technology evolved so did the course content and the mediums used, leading to the birth of AESL's Ed-Tech thrust. Slowly but surely, several innovative modules of technology-led programmes were added to the initial offerings.

Besides the extremely engaging lectures by the founder recorded on evolving digital devices, AESL introduced the format of an online classroom that also allowed students living in distant locales to interact with professors based in the head office in Delhi. This practice became the norm during the pandemic-stricken years of 2020 and 2021. It was introduced as early as in 2014 by Aakash in a bid to reach out to students living in the remotest parts of the country.

Aakash Digital Learning emerged from the clear need to not just supplement the class-room experience through recorded video lectures and integrated tests and assessments, but also to let students study at their own pace. Strong forums like Aakash iTutor, which included online assessment and test series via the Aakash Test Management System and live interactive classes via Aakash Live, became the cornerstone of AESL's Ed-Tech growth. These programmes not only expanded the group's geographical reach beyond classrooms by allowing students to access remote learning but also enhanced the in-class learning experience. The brilliant tech team at AESL mastered the use of audio-visual technology to make lectures interactive and interesting. This worked especially well while addressing the easily distracted youngsters who enrolled in the Foundation Programme.

"Aakash Live is an interactive virtual classroom which replicates a real classroom with the help of web real-time communication technology, delivered through tablets, mobile devices and laptops. In an Aakash Live classroom, our faculty members deliver lectures online," says Aakash. And in keeping with the egalitarian ethos of the group, this feature is sold individually to students as part of their coaching

Helming an enterprise that is worth a whopping seventy eight hundred crore rupees today, J.C. Chaudhry remembers every moment of his tough initial struggle. (Roy Henderson)

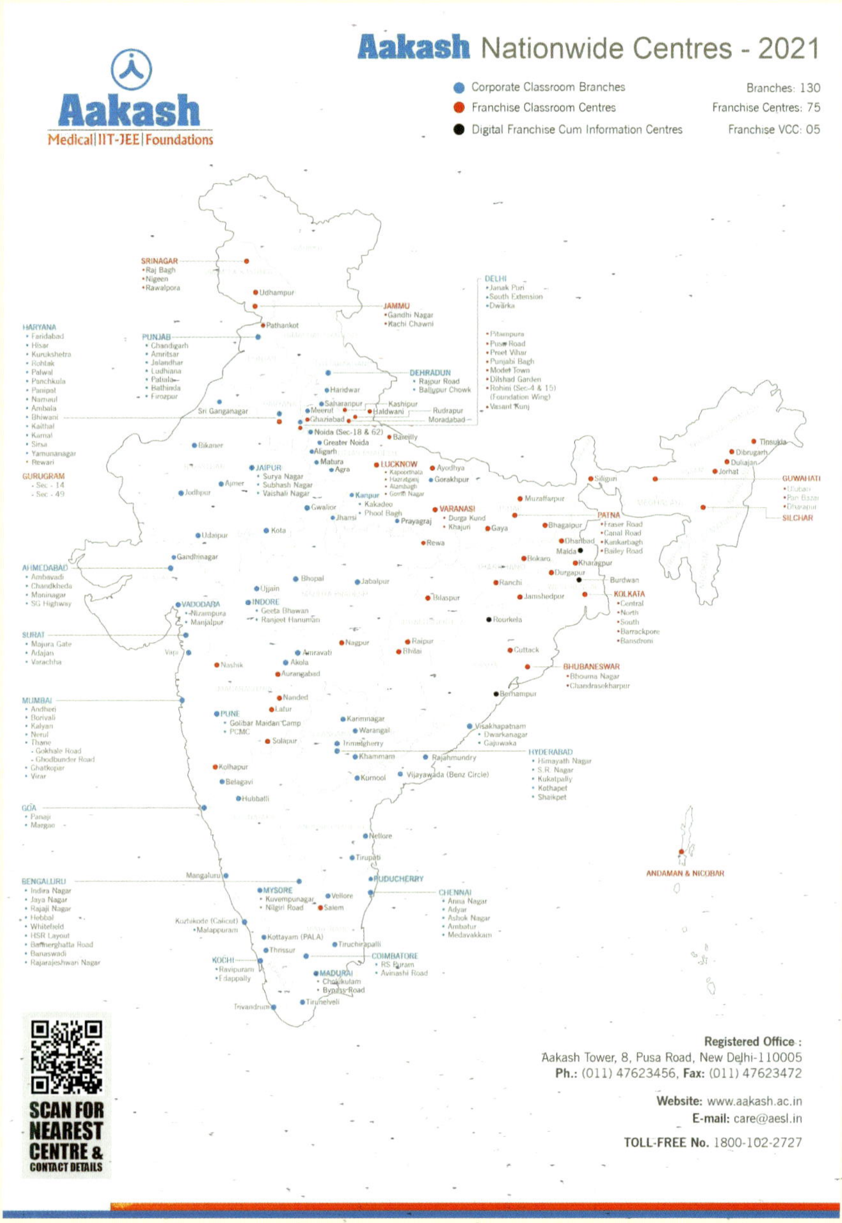

Aakash Educational Services Limited, India's largest chain of coaching centres, has introduced innovative, game-changing practices in education.

Left: 2020 NEET-UG All India Rank 7, Satwik Godara, Aakashian.
Bottom left: 2020 NEET-UG All India Rank 2, Akansha Singh, Aakashian
Bottom right: 2020 NEET-UG All India Rank 3, S. Nikitha Tummala, Aakashian.
©J.C. Chaudhry

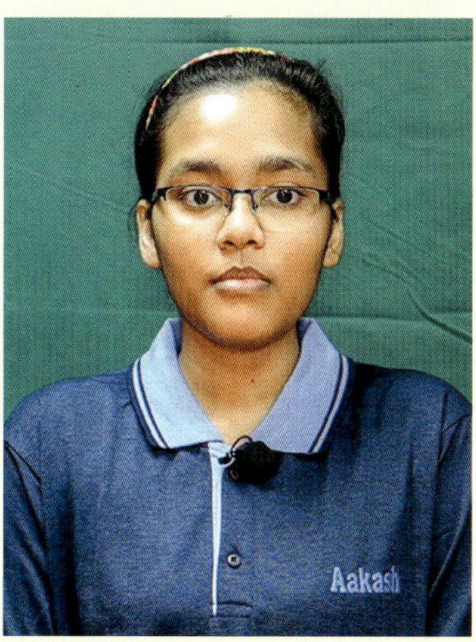

J.C. Chaudhry felicitating Aakashians Kalpana Kumari (2018 NEET-UG All India Rank 1), Akshat Kaushik (2019 NEET-UG All India Rank 3) and Sayantan Dhar (2019 IIT-JEE All India Rank 51). ©J.C. Chaudhry

J.C. Chaudhry felicitating Aakashians Bhavik Bansal (2019 NEET-UG All India Rank 2), Prateek Chaudhury (2019 IIT-JEE All India Rank 26) and Chirag Falor (2020 IIT-JEE All India Rank 1). ©J.C. Chaudhry

A teacher at heart, J.C. Chaudhry has the brain and brawn of an entrepreneur. He had the vision to monetise his teaching skills and turn his gift into a business opportunity. (Roy Henderson)

J.C Chaudhry and his two elder brothers, P.D. Chaudhry and J.D. Chaudhry, share a close bond. ©J.C. Chaudhry

J.C. Chaudhry (seen here addressing IIT students at Siri Fort Auditorium, Delhi, in 2019) aims to lead by example and inspire young people to believe in his own life's guiding motto: poverty is no bar to success. ©J.C. Chaudhry

An impressive speaker, J.C. Chaudhry (seen here addressing students at PHD Chamber, Delhi, in 2018) motivates the youth through inspirational talks where he shares experiences from his own life and the mantras of success he relies on. ©J.C. Chaudhry

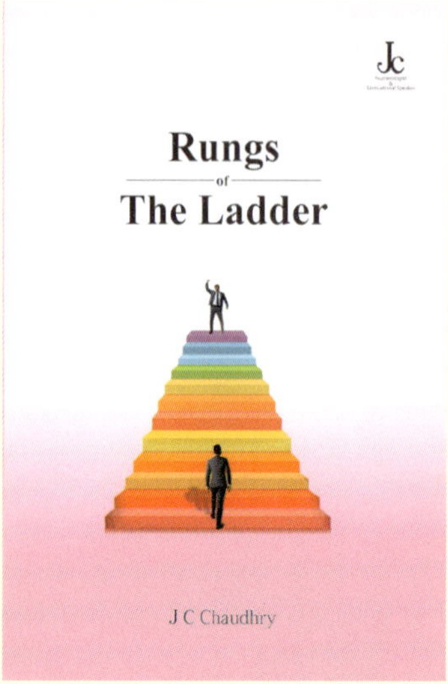

Delving deep into his vast storehouse of knowledge, J.C. Chaudhry shares insightful tips to cultivate mind control skills and elaborates on their practical applications in his books. These help readers thrive in their personal and professional lives. ©J.C. Chaudhry

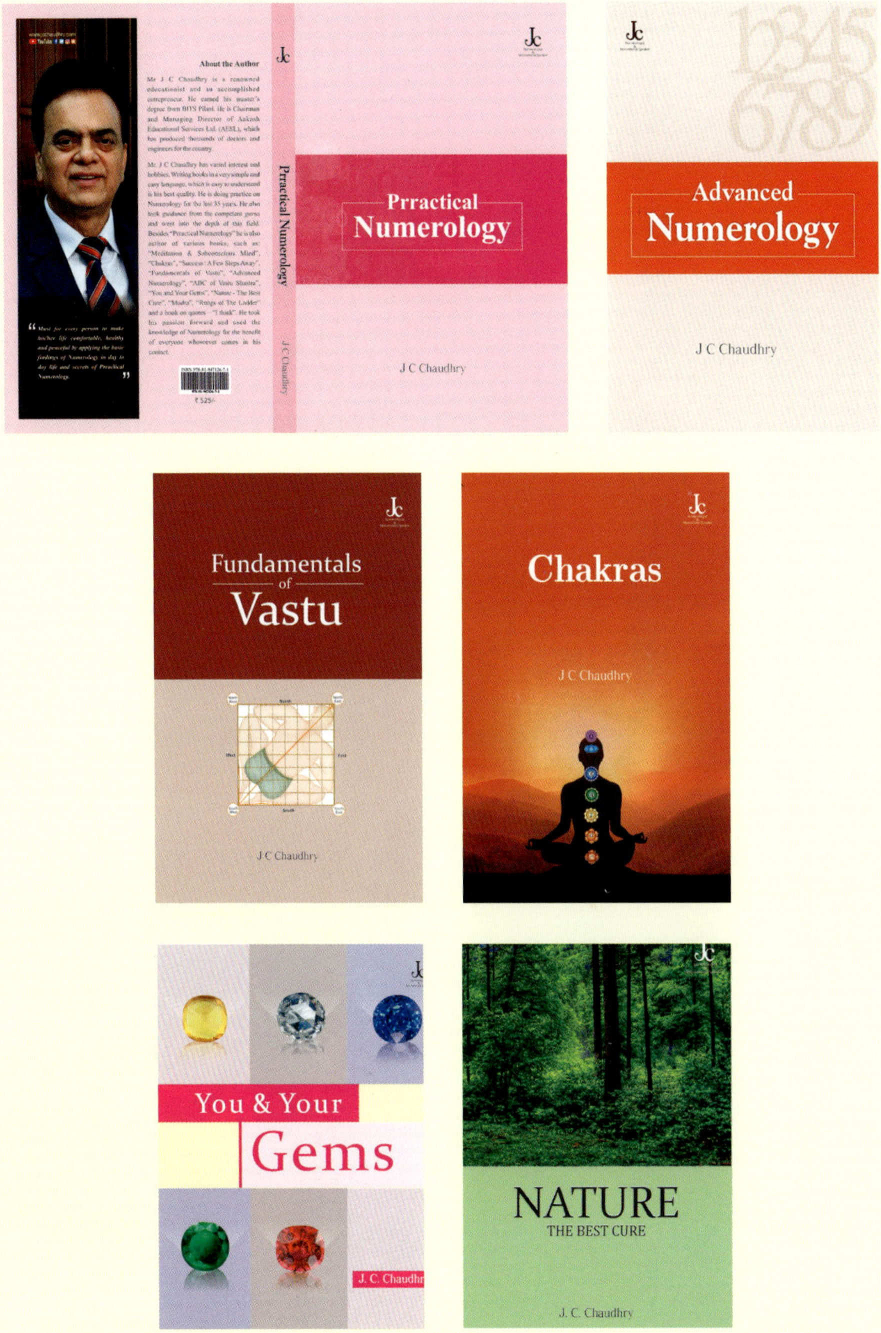

Books written by J.C Chaudhry cover an impressive range of topics including numerology, the impact of gems on the fate of humans and ways to calm the mind using the sublime tool of meditation. ©J.C. Chaudhry

J.C. Chaudhry considers his wife Kamla Chaudhry his biggest inspiration and source of support. The couple's bond is steadfast and their compatibility is reflected in all their joint decisions through the years.
(*Roy Henderson*)

J.C. Chaudhry discusses business moves threadbare with Aakash and Aashish. They latch on to his every word, placing their trust in his instincts and leadership philosophy. (Roy Henderson)

J.C. Chaudhry (daadu) with grandson Aayaan. ©J.C. Chaudhry

JC (daadu) with granddaughter Ashvika. ©J.C. Chaudhry

The Chaudhry clan is a close-knit unit living under one roof, always there to contribute and stand by each other in good times and bad. (*Roy Henderson*)

Both Aashish and Aakash Chaudhry were brought up to be independent and dynamic people. The senior Chaudhrys worked hard to make sterling men out of their sons. (Roy Henderson)

(Roy Henderson)

J.C. Chaudhry dotes on his four grandchildren: Aayaan, Ashvika, Aerika and Anyesha. At peace with himself, he gives them his undivided attention these days. (Roy Henderson)

J.C. Chaudhry and Kamla Chaudhry find the company of their grandchildren delightful. Happily retired now, J.C. Chaudhry spends a great deal of his time with them. @ J.C. Chaudhry

Having handed over the reins of his empire to his sons, J.C. Chaudhry now plays the role of Chairman Emeritus, and friend and guide to students who join Aakash Institute every year. (Roy Henderson)

package, and also made available to them through educational institutions. These virtual classrooms in schools provide access to students who have enrolled in Aakash Live but lack the devices to access the course material at their homes.

The fact that the Aakash Live platform takes the test-prep experience to far-flung regions, which were confined to the fringes, pleases Jagdish the most. Aakash, the management expert, sees great merit in this expanded geographical reach that helps the brand to forge ahead through the effective and efficient use of AESL's faculty. Besides, the modest cost of setting up an Aakash Live classroom keeps expenses low, allowing AESL to reach out to locations where setting up full-fledged Aakash centres is not economically viable.

While Aakash Live creates virtual classrooms, Aakash iTutor is a digital content-based platform providing recorded video lectures with integrated test-taking and self-assessment modules designed for self-paced learning. Marketed through tele-sales and at the many Aakash centres, this android app had over a million installations before the Covid-19 pandemic struck. When the pandemic-related lockdown set it, the numbers shot up since students who were homebound were forced to prepare remotely for their entrance tests.

Though perceived by Jagdish as blessings from Saraswati, the Goddess of learning, these online platforms do not satiate a child's need for real-time interaction, which has always been Aakash Institute's USP. No matter how clear the messaging, how interactive the lecture and how real the classroom, an intelligent mind buzzes with doubts that need clarification through face-to-face interactions. Aakash iCampus was introduced to close this gap. The initiative enhances the regular classroom experience and supplements classroom offerings using real-time tests, active feedback to both students and faculty members and increases interaction.

With the help of a digital database, the core group of senior faculty at Aakash addresses the queries of multiple students on a real-time basis in an automated environment, which collects information based on past data. The tech team is now in the process of creating a digital data bank of questions using inputs from the Aakash Live, Aakash iTutor and classroom platforms to build the Ask-an-Expert platform. "This service is intended to be an interactive guide for the student through a stand-alone application designed by a team consisting of faculty members, co-ordination members, product managers and an outsourced technology team," says Aakash.

Connected Classrooms allows students to interact one-on-one with a specific faculty member and clear their doubts through live streaming of the lecture. Aakash Test Learning Management System provides online test-taking services for self-assessment purposes, giving students a chance to benchmark their calibre against prevailing standards nationally. The AESL student count for Aakash digital learning offerings (for Aakash Live and Aakash iTutor) has increased from 3,208 in FY 2016 to 7,701 in FY 2018, growing at a CAGR (Compound Annual Growth Rate) of 54.94%.

Standardisation of not just procedures but course content is vital to technology-led education. AESL, under the wise guidance of their founder had the foresight to set up a core group of faculty in the corporate office. First guided by Jagdish and then by Aakash, this core committee creates content, which is error free and constantly updated. A National Academic Team of about seventy three faculty members monitors the entire bouquet of academic services and student performance as well. Be it an Aakashian in far-flung Jalpaiguri or the buzzing metropolis of Delhi, the Team is on hand to do the needful. The skilled academic team based in Delhi generates and upgrades content, selects and appraises faculty, training them regularly. Their most important role is to standardise coaching methods to ensure that a well-organised process is in place.

The excellent quality of course material gives Aakash Tutorials its greatest edge. "Study materials are prepared by our dedicated National Academic Team for all Aakash Medical, Aakash IIT-JEE and Aakash Foundation courses. They create centralised content, in consultation with classroom-centre teaching experts, using reference materials to ensure that syllabi of various subjects are addressed in an efficient and easy-to-understand manner. We begin by creating and updating test papers and our various study materials. Then, we digitise and edit them. Past exams are the biggest resource for our course creation," explains Aakash.

The study material contains illustrative theory and application-based questions which simplify the learning process. The material includes questions and corresponding answers. Summarised answers, crisp questions, and engaging illustrations are all also translated for the online white board experience. In addition to this, a blend of classroom and online learning courses such as the Aakash Hybrid Programme is designed to ensure a seamless experience for students who can prepare long distance all through their foundation years and step into the classroom closer to the dates of the entrance tests.

Jagdish is fairly tech savvy himself. In the midst of the pandemic, he launched his JC Nummerro App that was overwhelmed with downloads the moment it was online. The devoted numerologist combined his thirty five years of complex and layered experience in the science of numerology with the linear functionality of technology insisting that even though he was "born in an era when owning a radio set was more invigorating than a space ship", he feels technology is the only way forward. And this holds especially true when it comes to adapting technology to education, given the way it levels the field in terms of accessibility for more aspirants.

Jagdish is very proud of the unique collaboration between Airtel Digital TV, the DTH arm of Bharti Airtel and AESL that launched in October 2020 India's first dedicated TV channel for medical and engineering entrance exams preparation. "Now, at a mere Rs. 247 a month, our Foundation and JEE courses are made available exclusively on Airtel Digital TV. You have no idea how many students have benefitted from this. Aakash and I personally handpick our best faculty who teach these students through LIVE interactive classes, helping them to learn key concepts and solve problems," says Jagdish.

The sessions help aspirants living in far-flung areas to avail of the same quality of coaching a JEE-aspirant based in metropolitan cities such as Delhi and Mumbai would have access to. The programme transcends geographical boundaries and does away with the dependence on the Internet and access to technology. It proved to be a big boon during the Covid-19 pandemic period. Jagdish realised his dream of coaching, counselling and guiding children from rural and economically weak backgrounds in pursuing their careers through this programme.

Widely advertised in rural India, this is a gender-sensitive programme as it allows girls to settle down before the television set to study while the smart phone is monopolised by the boys in the family. "It breaks my heart to see that the norm in villages is still that sons must be educated while the daughters can get married and be 'settled'. In this light, I am glad that we have made it possible for girls who are aspiring to be doctors and engineers to study at home," says Jagdish who insists that education has to be made available to anyone who is hungry for knowledge.

~

K-12 or Kindergarten to Class 12 is the largest segment of education. India's education industry was estimated at 8,400–8,600 billion rupees (USD 130–135 billion) in FY 2018. The formal K-12 and higher education segments have a lion's share of the market, while the coaching and test-preparatory segments together account for 27%. The industry grew at a 15% rate and is projected to grow with a Compound Annual Growth Rate (CAGR) of 14% over the next three years. Between FY 2013 and 2018, the non-formal segment notched a growth of 17% CAGR whereas the formal segment, which accounts for approximately two-thirds of the sector, grew at a CAGR of 13%. CRISIL Research expects the industry to grow at a healthy CAGR of 14% over the next three years with the share of different segments in the education industry likely to remain more or less stable. Currently, India is one of the nations with the highest population of the young, with a median age of twenty eight years. CRISIL Research expects that the existence of a large share of this age group, coupled with rapid urbanisation and rising affluence, will give rise to a huge demand for the K-12 education segment in India.

AESL enjoys the lion's share of the test-prep market, especially in the brick-and-mortar format with exemplary results in medical and engineering entrance exams. Jagdish attributes this success to the foundation course that scouts for talent through a many-layered selection process and starts talking to aspirants in as early as at the Class 9 phase when they are fifteen years old. Jagdish believes that their minds are mouldable and eager to learn and if you set them in the right direction at that age, acing an exam after they complete Class 12 becomes easier."

Besides, competitive examinations like the International Mathematics Olympiad, National Science Olympiad and National Talent Search Examination (NTSE) provide a great platform for students to develop their analytical skills and master Mathematics and Science. These also act as a sound foundation for candidates planning to prepare for the Joint Entrance Examination (JEE) and the National Eligibility Cum Entrance Test (NEET) later on in life. The willingness on the part of students to start preparing for the entrance exams as well as the school-level Board exams from an early age, coupled with increasing awareness among parents about the need to prepare their children at a young age for these exams has led to increased enrollment in AESL's foundation courses.

Started in 2009, the well-rounded Foundation Course at AESL is offered both online and in the classroom. The younger computer savvy generation relies heavily on both the online courses and classroom-led coaching. The AESL faculty creates impressive course material, offering focused test-preparatory courses to students of Classes 9 and 10. AESL has also custom created a focused test-preparatory course for fourteen year olds stepping into Class 8. This is offered to them via Aakash Live. Whilst the focus is on providing training to these students for the central and state Board examinations, emphasis is also laid on giving them an edge in junior competitive scholarship tests and merit tests such as the Olympiads and National Talent Search Examination (NTSE).

Jagdish says, "Exams are a must to train your mind and discipline your response to help you complete the test in a stipulated time frame. Students have to start honing their skills in giving competitive exams early on." AESL has seen a steady increase in the enrollment of their

Foundation Course which grew from a student count of 25,899 in 2016 to 33,718 in 2017 and to 43,058 in 2018.

Foundation courses focusing on subjects including Science, Mathematics, English and Social Sciences aim to initiate students into mastering the art of giving exams. The undergraduate test preparatory coaching institutes have recorded a growing demand for foundation courses in the last five years. CRISIL Research clocks this growth to over rupees 390 billion by the end of 2021.

A coaching centre is as successful as its last good result. As exams got tougher, it became even more important to find the right candidate to train and prepare for the tough task ahead. Hence, the students who enrolled in the foundation courses also turned into the captive market for the medical and engineering entrance exams. Along with streamlining the coaching processes internally, Aakash began to feel the need to innovate the outreach plan of AESL. He wanted to find a way to reach out to and enroll the brightest minds into their programme, hence strengthening the chance of producing great results in the competitive exams.

Coaching institutions were not in the habit of hand-picking their students. AESL changed this by introducing entrance and scholarship tests that have become national benchmarks today. The core committee of management and faculty decided to recognise and reward passionate and talented students across the nation with up to 100% scholarships, based on the result of the scholarship tests the students would be put through. This would give brilliant and deserving students a great opportunity to kickstart their journey and get admitted to courses of their choice. The scholarship tests that AESL conducts includes the Admission cum Scholarship Test (ACST), the Aakash National Talent Hunt Examination (ANTHE) and, launched most recently, the Aakash Talent Quest (ATQ).

"We believe in discovering and nurturing talent. Towards this end, we follow a multi-pronged and detailed admission process, which starts with an organised format for collecting data on prospective students. This is done through very intense marketing programmes. We conduct seminars at schools, hold counselling sessions in prominent middle-class colonies, advertise in local media, contact prospective students and invite them to seminars held at our centres. We also encourage branch visits by prospective students who meet with our team and avail of counselling before enrollment," says Aakash.

The scholarship tests are the first hurdles many bright students cross. They give students a chance to assess their performance based on their ranking on the merit list, and many students who take these tests subsequently enroll in Aakash. "When we introduced these exams, we were questioned, even mocked. How could a coaching centre 'select' students? But these tests let us to sift the grain from the chaff. They also give the faculty an idea about the students they should watch out for," says Jagdish. "For me, however, the biggest reward is giving 100% scholarships to needy students who go on to become doctors," he adds. "At Aakash Healthcare we have recruited a few scholarship-holding Aakashians who came from humble backgrounds and could only study for the entrance test because of our support."

Another innovative examination forum introduced by AESL is the All India Aakash Test Series. Conducted for students at Aakash centres across India, this exam prepares students for the entrance exams and offers them an opportunity test their calibre at the all-India level. This test is open to both Aakash and non-Aakash students and the questions are prepared by Aakash faculty members. The Aakash Test Series also helps the faculty at AESL to identify and attract students in Classes 11 and 12 who have the potential to score well. These bright students are then offered lucrative scholarships and invited to enroll in their desired stream, be it medicine or engineering. And besides, this national-level exam helps the core faculty team to gauge which centres in the long list of coaching colleges under the AESL umbrella need to beef up their test-giving acumen.

Raindrops make a river and many rivers come together make the ocean. Over the years, the hard-working, visionary father and his enterprising son built AESL brick by brick and made it the shining star it is today. It thrives and touches new heights due to their constant innovation.

11

Forays Into Healthcare

Jagdish calls his elder son his replica, seeing in him the same fire and drive that he himself had during his formative years. They share the need to achieve and a similar steadfast vision to grow. In fact, he often refers to Aashish as a volcano waiting to erupt or the next big thing to happen to the group. Admittedly, Aashish has always been his soft spot right from the day he was born with a club foot, plunging his parents into the depths of despair and anguish. The daunting struggle that followed further strengthened that bond.

However, this did not stop the father from using the same prudence in Aashish's upbringing as he did for his younger son, Aakash. However, despite the iron fist, Aashish remained in total awe of his father, closely observing how he 'made doctors,' hoping that he would one day make his father proud by becoming one himself. He was witness to the pride Jagdish felt every time an Aakashian became a doctor and he too wanted to be one and impress his father.

This thought was further aided by the father's constant subliminal suggestions in that direction. He wanted his son to be a doctor and he motivated him in that direction. Knowing the tough road ahead, the strict father got stricter with him. Aashish is in fact convinced that his father was more liberal with the stick than the carrot when it came to his upbringing. "I got my younger brother's share of brick bats too being the elder child. But this strictness ended with discipline and if I was in trouble then he was right by my side, ready with his kind, listening ear and loving shoulder."

Seeing him blossom into a respected orthopedic surgeon, a Fellow at the Royal College of Surgeons of Glasgow, and Founder of Aakash Healthcare that puts preventive action at par with cure is Jagdish's childhood dream of becoming a doctor vicariously come true. Whilst Aakash turned into his father's trusted partner, Aashish took the solitary journey in the world of medicine, honing himself to be a 'doctorpreneur' and mastering the complex realm of knee surgery which he conducts today with robotic assistance. The journey was quiet eventful and a showcase of Aashish's capacity for hard work that he insists he has inherited from his father. "I am a replica of him," he says proudly.

On completing his Masters in orthopedic surgery from Lady Harding Medical College in 2007, Aashish began working in a government hospital. It was a long drawn out journey: three years of training, three years of senior residency, followed by two years of fellowship. During this time he was introduced to his future wife Meinal, a radiologist as career oriented as him. It was Jagdish's old mentor, Tanejaji, who had suggested his niece as a potential match for Aashish. Aashish and Meinal hit it off and their families arranged a grand wedding for them. The Chaudhrys welcomed their new daughter with open arms into the family.

For the first few years Meinal and Aashish worked at Safdarjung Hospital, earning a comfortable salary. Parents of a baby girl, Ashvika, they were happy, content and enjoying a set routine of hospital, home, family and friends. Aashish, however, knew that this was just goalpost number one in his career. He had to get back to the apprentice life and learn the finer, newer nuances of surgery from an experienced person. Medicine like law is a career that calls for constant updating of one's skills and keeping up with technology.

Aashish was introduced to a legendary surgeon through a friend (the surgeon's apprentice) who was moving on and had decided to offer the job to Aashish. The surgeon, a Padma Shri winner had operated on the knees of celebrities like Virender Sehwag and V.S. Naipul and had a formidable reputation. Aashish was over the moon at the prospect of assisting him and learning from him in the process. He even mentally prepared himself to take a salary cut if necessary.

Aashish stepped into the surgeon's newly furbished, swanky clinic in one of South Delhi's upmarket colonies. He was there on his own merit, an aspiring surgeon in search of an apprenticeship. As usual he refrained from revealing the fact that he was a scion of the Aakash empire and son of the legendary teacher who was responsible for setting so many doctors on their career paths. The senior surgeon was preparing a presentation for a talk he was to give the next day. He sat Aashish down and glanced around the clinic, pointedly asking Aashish if he had ever seen such a great clinic and adding that a young surgeon like him would be lucky to be working with a legend like him.

Aashish, though a little taken aback by the "air of arrogance," humbly expressed his gratitude and deep desire to be his assistant. He promised that he would put in his heart and soul into the job and prove to be an asset. He assured him that he would not look at the hours he spent there or the effort put in. All he requested was that he be paid an apprentice's salary, which would be much less than what he was currently earning. To his surprise, the surgeon heard him out and refused to support him monetarily, expecting him to work as a locum. He countered that Aashish could not be expected to get paid when he was this opportunity to work and learn from a surgeon of such repute.

The sheer arrogance of it hit Aashish hard. He walked out of the clinic battling a volley of emotions. He was angry, low on self-esteem, depressed and restless. However, this episode had revved up his "settled" adrenaline and got him all charged up to "be someone, do something." He was dismayed at discovering how senior doctors were treating young fellows. If he, from an urbane, Delhi background could be dealt with so high handedly, how must other doctors from small towns and humble backgrounds be treated? This meeting taught him that no matter how accomplished he became he must never occupy a pedestal and break a young doctor's spirit.

Aashish shared the incident with his father who sensed his restlessness. The hero once again rose to the occasion, soothing his son's frayed nerves. Jagdish suggested that it was time for Aashish to go solo and helm his own practice. He offered to help his son build his own clinic. Jagdish had invested in an institutional land for a hospital in Dwarka that he got at a DDA auction in 2006 for eight crore rupees. In the same vicinity, he had also invested in a large commercial building situated in a well inhabited area. Using the top three floors as an office of AESL, he had left the basement and ground floor of the building empty. He had hoped that one day, this spot located in the heart of the colony would work very well as his son's clinic—a thought he had kept to himself. Both his sons had to be self-made men. Offering them things on a platter would kill their drive as young professionals.

Even when Aashish came back to him hurt but keen to stand on his own feet, Jagdish applied a jurist's prudence while offering the space to Aashish. He asked him, in a businesslike manner, to first spell out the ROI (Return of Investment) if he were to use such a large space as a clinic where he would not get more than three to four patients a day. He added that it would be a bad idea to hold up a 4,000 square feet space that would fetch him a substantial rent otherwise. Aashish pleaded his case, promising to grow the business with his hard work and make the clinic earn a profit, justifying the rental lost. Pleased with his answer, Jagdish handed over the space to Aashish, adding in his characteristic style that he was not allowed to use the brand name 'Aakash' for his clinic till he had proven his mettle as a surgeon to the world!

~

Jagdish has a knack for investing in property in a thorough and well-researched manner. His firm view is that one should never buy a piece of land that is of no real business or personal use. Also, never invest in a property outside the city you reside in. What you can't personally oversee is best left alone. This theory stood him in great stead, accelerating the growth of his education empire. AESL today leases most of its addresses, making mobility from one venue to the other easy and also minimising the capital allocated in setting up a centre, which makes the multiplication game easier. In any case, the coaching industry in comparison to health care is less capital intensive. All you need is the wherewithal to be able to take a building on rent, furnish it with desks, tables and technology and then have enough savings to pay salaries to teaching and non-teaching staff till the fees earned from students pay for it. With no land bought and fancy buildings built, Aakash centres could afford to literally mushroom across the country.

The clinic, however, needed machines, furniture, labs and a few assistants to start with. Aashish took a seed fund from his father and got down to work. He hired Sanjay Makhija, the same architect who had designed all the Aakash centres and knew how to deliver quickly. He asked Sanjay to first visit the senior surgeon's swanky clinic and absorb the space. He wanted his clinic to be the best in the market. The architect zipped across town to the surgeon's clinic under the pretext of getting his ligament tested, and took a good look at the decor and design of the space. He was ready to build Aashish's clinic and make it a unique place. He submitted a blue print in a week and Aashish was pleased because this was exactly how he had envisioned his clinic. Aashish gave it the generic name of Bone and Joint Clinic and on 11 November, 2011, (which as per numerology was an auspicious 11-11-11), and his clinic was born.

Now began the acid test of making a name for himself in this middle-class colony which functioned like a self-sufficient island. Inhabited by white collar workers, small-time businessmen, government employees and young professionals, Dwarka already had a good roster of physicians, specialists and surgeons. Residents had their own favourite doctors whom they patronised and consulted. Aashish had to break into that comfort zone and get people to look beyond their favourites. The idea he came up with to do this was ingenious and called for relentless hard work.

Every Sunday, he would keep his clinic open while the forty other orthopedic surgeons practising in the area were taking a siesta. Bones don't take holidays, nor do falls or accidents. Hence, anyone who had a broken bone or a hurting cartilage, sought help and discovered Aashish Chaudhry's Bone and Joint Clinic that stayed open on Sundays. Better still the patients were greeted by the surgeon himself who immediately put them at ease. Soon enough the existing bastions were breached and trust was won.

Patients began pouring in daily and Dr. Aashish built a good reputation. He turned his clinic into a 24/7 consultancy. No matter what time of the day or night, he would rush back from his home in Vasant Vihar, which was quite a distance away, if he had to attend to a patient. Interestingly, three months later, the senior surgeon who had refused to pay him a salary called him and asked him to reconsider working with him. This time he even offered him a "small salary" and said that offers like these did not come by every day. And besides, how much could he be making out of a tiny clinic in a tony colony! Aashish gracefully turned him down.

"Getting rejected that day was the best thing that happened to me. Otherwise who knows, I would still be working for someone. The experience fired me up to prove my own worth," says Aashish. Soon, he had four junior surgeons working for him. He hired all of them on merit and politely refused those who did not fit in with his work style. Within two years he had built both a reputation and a repertoire of patients. He now began thinking of working on a blue print of a hospital that would keep good practice at the heart of its service. He prepared a full presentation to plead his case before his father.

Jagdish meanwhile had decided it was time to allow his son to not just use his brand name for the clinic but also begin planning for a full-fledged healthcare facility with orthopedics at its core. He was receiving glowing reports on Aashish, the surgeon. Many of his friends and associates who had been operated upon by his son had applauded Aashish's surgical prowess. The young surgeon had also operated upon many of the members of his family. When he was still an apprentice, he had been asked to do a complex hip replacement surgery on his grandfather. He operated on his mother's ankle when she slipped at their temple in Vrindavan, knee replacement procedures on Meinal's mother and Aakash's mother-in-law. Most importantly, he took on his father's knee replacement surgery with which he literally inaugurated the operation theatre at the hospital.

Jagdish, a believer in Ayurveda and natural healing, had tried everything: ancient medicines, therapeutic massages with pain oils, etc. Eventually, he agreed to go under the knife as long as Aashish operated on him. Jagdish was as much in awe of Aashish the surgeon as he was of his classmate, Dr. Bhature who could dissect a pigeon's arteries with precision and had been given the privilege to operate on baby Aashish's clubfoot eons ago.

~

A sensible father, Jagdish knew the merits of helping to create individual career paths for his sons, allocating family resources in equal measure to help them both stand on their own feet. An intelligent leader, he also knew how to invest his hard-earned money wisely. Above all, when allocating capital, he was intuitive enough to look at businesses, like education that will never go 'out of business'. Healthcare, hence, hefelt was a logical brand extension for AESL. It was a well-thoughtout foray into a terrain that was new for him but a perfect direction to take. Given the fact that the family now had two doctors who wanted to usher in a positive change in the medical profession, this made perfect sense.

Jagdish had a keen, scholarly interest in the world of wellness himself. A professor of Botany and Zoology he was able to connect the human body to nature's bounty and how the latter enriched the former's wellbeing. He also wrote a book on the subject titled *Nature, the Best Cure*. An avid yoga exponent, a self-taught nutritionist and also a firm believer in the motto that prevention is better than cure, he decided to work with his elder son to create a healthcare facility, which viewed healthcare holistically. He wished to create a temple of healing where people gave wellness the importance it deserves and learnt to live a truly healthy life. His favourite saying being, "We would love it if your good health puts us out of business!"

With Aashish, he dreamt of not just creating one of the first iconic super specialty hospitals in Dwarka, Delhi, but also making some paradigm shifts in prevailing health care practices. This business endeavour also became an opportunity to partner with his elder son, and venture into an arena beyond the realm of education in which Aashish had little interest.

Father and son shared a collective vision of creating a health care service that was ethical above all and had the well being of the patient at its core. Jagdish proved to be a very useful partner for his son, offering valuable inputs into myriad aspects of building a world-class health care facility. Right from holding meetings the architects who designed the facility to accompanying Aashish in the procurement of equipment and machinery to hiring staff who would share their collective vision of bringing positive change and planning the customer outreach, marketing and advertising, he was involved with it all. Aashish relied heavily on his father to select the right candidates for the venture. He agreed with his father that one bad fish could dirty the entire pond.

Both of them shared the vision of creating a healthcare facility where medicine is practised as nobly and freely as it is supposed to be. The crucial belief being that health care must focus on preventive action as well as research and development. A science professor himself, Jagdish also believed in medicine being an ever-evolving practice making it imperative for the facility to be abreast with global practices in health care.

The hospital business is a capital intensive one. It calls for a lot of patience and money power to wait it out. Unlike an educational institute, hospitals call for state-of-the-art operation theatres, Intensive Care Units, OPD, IPD facility, sophisticated machines such as X-ray machines, laser machines and CAT scan units. Jagdish was clear that no stone be left unturned and no technological breakthroughs missed. No obsolete systems were to be bought in order to save on expenses. Aakash Healthcare's first address had to make the established names in healthcare sit up and take notice. Father and son personally oversaw each machine that was added, and every room that was fixed up. They were determined to make the health-care facility at par with any across the globe in terms of infrastructure.

Aakash Healthcare, as the name suggests, was positioned as a brand extension of AESL, India's leading education empire. Brand extensions mostly work when the new enterprise remains within the industry purview of the original business, the reputation of the parent brand rubbing off on the fledgling, giving it a base to take off from. AESL, however, had a subliminal link to medicine. Many doctors who were recruited to the facility were Aakashians and already a fan of Chaudhry Sir. The medical community knew of Aakash and linked it to quality, honesty and gravitas. This helped Aashish to initially hand pick the best doctors. For this task, he relied heavily on his father's instincts and unique ability to gauge people's characters. Aashish calls his father Jahanpanah (emperor) of the family. His father's decisions are steadfast and respected by the entire family. Addressing his father more often as Chairman Sir than dad he constantly looks up to him for adding intellectual depth to his vision.

When Aashish was formalising the vision and mission of the healthcare facility, his father asked him to place service before profits. He assured Aashish that God had been kind to their family and had blessed them with enough money to live a comfortable life. The only thing he had to ensure that the hospital always took the honest and kind route. At the same time, it had to be a self-sustaining enterprise and not become a liability to the parent company.

He requested Aashish to create a facility that brought back the glory of the profession of medicine. Aashish was very impressed. It was incredible that a man who had begun his journey with a monthly salary of 446 rupees and struggled to get to where he had now reached, was telling him to put service before profit. He felt blessed to be born to a man of such vision. "My father means the world to me. All I need in life is his approval and once he gives a nod to a decision of mine, I do not care what the rest of the world thinks," he shares. And so he decided to create a perfect world where doctors were free to practice their profession and not be under any pressure to add to the profitability of the hospital. A decision that literally gave him and his colleagues wings to fly.

The hospital doors were thrown open to the public on 27 August, 2017. On the first day of OPD itself, they had 188 registrations which exceeded the tally of many established and seasoned brands. Aakash's clinic had already made a name for itself locally thanks to the meticulous brand-building exercise that focused on serving the people living in and around Dwarka. The ripple effect of trusting the hospital was a natural corollary to this. It took the hospital a short span of fifteen months to break even and Aakash Healthcare was lauded for its commitment to honest medical practices.

Jagdish conceived the hospital as a place where doctors did not feel like employees but partners who had collaborated with the management's vision to serve people. This was a facility that did not recommend surgeries unnecessarily or order expensive tests when not needed. In short, the doctors were free to function with no turnover targets. They did not worry about ensuring that the hospital earned a certain amount regularly. Aashish, a doctor first, welcomed this decision made by his father. It was his dream as well to create a place where treatment is for the sake of cure and not for adding to the bottom line. Doctors should not be treated as profit machines, he was clear about this. They were messiahs who heal the world. To make this dream real, it was important to hire not just competent doctors but also those who shared this view of being the change they wanted to see in the world. They could never forget their pledge to treat and heal without any bias.

This magnanimous theory came into good use during the pandemic of 2020 and 2021 when the hospital was overwhelmed with a flood of patients. Aashish and his father introduced certain practices during this crisis. These were not just path breaking but also humane at the core. Having suffered from Covid-19 himself in March 2020 when the world was treating it as a fearful Frankenstein, Aashish knew, first hand, the psychological trauma the disease causes. He had seen its affects up close. The inability of meeting your loved ones, the helplessness of seeing yourself collapse and facing a solitary end was a reality that could daunt the bravest. Even the nursing staff felt vulnerable and exposed.

The Chaudhrys were clear that both the patients and staff had to be dealt with utmost kindness. Every patient was fed by hand by the nurses. The staff called the patients' families every evening giving them an honest and detailed progress report of their loved one. The staff was allowed to stay in the guest house and served all meals. Their families received full rations for the months, given that their loved ones were unable to get home. This produced commendable results. The hospital saw very few fatalities, even sending home five patients after they were on ventilators for sixty days. While service was their mantra, profits did not dwindle. Even in this crisis, Jagdish's karmic theory of what goes around comes around came true. Intent had preceded profit and the hospital's reputation for saving lives spread across the whole country.

Aakash Healthcare has brought about some paradigm shifts in current healthcare practices. To begin with, the word 'healthcare' and not 'hospital' in the name itself gives as much importance to prevention as to cure. Jagdish is convinced that no one wants to come to a hospital willingly. Hence, people should be helped to adopt a lifestyle that prevents them from doing so. A firm believer that only a healthy country can progress he calls it a patriotic act to shake the denizens out of their sedentary lifestyle that leads to many ailments. Diabetes, hypertension, thyroid, back pain all emerge from sitting around for long hours. So does the absence of daily walks and exercise.

Aashish points out that the hospital offers free medical camps to the community comprising of over forty lakh citizens who live in and around Dwarka. At these camps people are tested on the spot for lifestyle-related diseases. These tests often throw up alarming results like post-prandial sugar levels being 500 in twenty-seven-year-old boys. Jagdish personally oversees the CSR activities of the hospital under which mobile vans with medicines, doctors and nurses are dispatched to remote villages of Haryana and thousands of people offered primary healthcare.

On the growth front, Aashish is bullish, but not reckless. Inspired by the growth pace maintained by reputed Indian hospital chains like Apollo, which, like Aakash Healthcare is family run, Aashish is championing growth with a vision. He feels that the hospital, thanks to his father's vision, has been lucky from day one. He is now implementing his own plans to create hierarchies and management systems that will put the hospital on autopilot. Convinced that he has inherited both his management skills and intolerance to incompetence from his father, Aashish has built a competent administrative wing and a series of well-thoughtout and listed SOPs that make day-to-day functioning a smooth affair, leaving him free to focus on improving his surgery skills. Greatly influenced by the intervention of technology, this surgeon applies robotics to knee surgery. His acclaim as a knee surgeon has grown over time and he is forever grappling with a long waitlist of patients who only want to be operated upon by Dr. Aashish Chaudhry.

With a vision to grow, the group is now looking for brown field projects, adopting fully functional but obsolete hospital facilities that have all the compliances in place, a reputation at a local level and a solid roster of patients and doctors. Once acquired, these facilities get rebranded as Aakash Healthcare and the corporate team at Dwarka takes over to ensure the same level of services are offered at all these hospitals, big or small.

Aashish's heart though is set on his biggest dream. He has collaborated with the Hospital for Special Surgery (HSS), New York, the Mecca of orthopedic surgeons all over the world. The HSS specialises in orthopedic surgery and the treatment of rheumatologic conditions. Founded in 1863 by James Knight this is not just the oldest orthopedic hospital in the United States but one that has remained consistently the top orthopedic hospital in the country. Areas of expertise at HSS include joint replacement, orthopedic trauma, hand and upper extremity surgery, limb lengthening, foot and ankle surgery, pediatric orthopedics, spine surgery and sports medicine.

Of special interest to Aashish is the fact that the HSS performs the maximum number of knee replacement surgeries in the United States. The sports medicine services at the hospital treats athletic injuries of the muscular-skeletal system with a special focus on shoulder, elbow and knee injuries. Aakash Healthcare is all set to bring the facility to India and work has already begun in that direction at Gurugram. This move, to both father and son, is the advantage of having capital to use for value addition.

Father of two daughters, Aashvika and Anyesha, Aashish hopes they will eventually helm the administrative wing, revving it up with their own vision. He makes it clear that he does not want to influence them in any way when they choose their career paths. It should and will be their individual decision. But he would love them to take an interest in the healthcare business and commit themselves to its growth. "If they want to take this oath that is..." he adds.

His granddaughters are Jagdish's favourites. He dotes on them and Aashish and Meinal are touched to see the love he showers on them. Jagdish, happily retired now, spends a great deal of his time with them. This makes him immensely happy. Aashish is sad to note that his tiger, his Jahanpanah is growing old gradually and is happiest these days when he is writing books on spirituality or predicting the future using numerology. Jagdish also spends time with his equally spiritually inclined wife, overseeing the construction of the Chaar Dhaam at their temple in Lord Krishna's abode, Vrindavan. Seeing the tiger in this tame mode is both an invigorating and depressing sight for his elder son who has seen his father charge ahead all his life to protect his family and steer it through ups and downs with admirable grace.

12

Science And Spirituality

As a student, he ran away from mathematics, yet, numbers went on to become his best friends. J.C. Chaudhry is hailed as a legend in numerology today. His YouTube channel, loaded with a series of informative videos has a dedicated following of over 6,00,000 subscribers. Every video he posts elicits at least a million views. The website www.jcchaudhry.com has been visited by over eight crore people and the JC Numero App that he launched on 15 December, 2020 is flooded with subscriptions. His inbox is full of queries from troubled souls who want to find the way out of their troubles through numbers. Jagdish uses the power of numerology, a practice that dates back to the ancient civilisations of Atlantis, Babylon, Greece, China and India to unravel life's many puzzles. From financial issues, compatibility concerns or emotional issues, he is able to show the way to people grappling with problems of all types and magnitudes.

Jagdish is not just a great educator, lateral thinker and a believer of pure sciences. In his heart there is a place for spirituality, an undying trust in natural healing, mastery over Vastu and above all, a near perfect grasp of numerology. His persona can be compartmentalised into two: the self-made tycoon in the world of education and the spiritual believer who is a philanthropist at heart.

Act of kindnesses, which the corporate world calls CSR, come naturally to him. There are innumerable instances to cite such as the time he instantly donated money to his village, Hathin, to build a crematorium when he saw the village elders being cremated in the open in the middle of a field. He felt that he owed it to his village to ensure a proper funeral for them, and adequate space for the mourners to gather. He donated Rs. 10,00,000 to his fraternity of science teachers in Delhi to use for research and development. "Money is simply a means to an end," he says. "How you use it is up to you. Everyone uses their money for themselves, but sharing it with others is the real deal. I feel money is best put to use to improve people's lives." This philosophy also guided him to perfect his numerology expertise so he could help distressed and lost souls.

The generous numerologist spends every Sunday answering a heap of letters and emails that are painstakingly printed by his secretary and personally delivered to the people who write to him. While the world lazes around in siesta mode, Jagdish sits at his desk, upright, a printed letter on one side and a notepad on the other. He answers every question, dictating it to his man Friday who diligently sends Chairman Sir's reply to each and every seeker. This service has been rendered free of cost for the last thirty years.

Jagdish approaches numerology with the precision of a scientist and the thirst to learn. Speaking to eager audiences on a range of subjects like ways to save yourself from overthinking and tips to save your marriage, he sounds as inspiring as he does when delivering motivational lectures to Aakashians on the eve of their entrance exams. Everything he takes up is backed by deep knowledge and intense research.

How did a science teacher desperate to make ends meet get introduced to the practice of numerology? How he learnt its intricacies overnight is quite a tale. It happened quite as spontaneously as most things that he experienced in his life as a seeker. It all began nearly thirty five years ago when both his sons were very young and the Chaudhrys were residing in their rented accommodation in West Delhi. One Sunday morning, an advocate and a friend of Jagdish's woke the entire neighbourhood up by honking incessantly outside their door. He asked

Jagdish to pack a bag and also bring along his family as he was driving to Haridwar and wanted to take them all with him. Jagdish, Kamla and their two children got dressed and drove towards the holy city where the Ganges flows quietly. Their destination was the pristine and pious world residing on its shore, enveloped in its energy and warmth.

Jagdish's brother-in-law, Y.K. Gauba lived in Ranipur, BHEL's township in Haridwar developed in the 1960s as part of then Prime Minister Jawahar Lal Nehru's dream of setting up factories in townships with holy shrines as, 'Temples of Modern India'. Jagdish insisted that they stay with him after they took the holy dip at Hari-ki-Paudi, the steps that flank the gushing Ganga, allowing devotees to take a holy dip while clinging to the iron rails erected near the steps. It is from these very steps that devotees witness the ethereal Ganga aarti, in which thousands of diyas (small lamps) placed aboard boats float on the river.

Tired but content they reached Ranipur in time for dinner. After dinner, Gauba casually shared with Jagdish something he had learnt while he was posted at Hyderabad. He had met a renowned numerologist there and been fascinated by the practice. He talked to Jagdish in detail about numerology, how numbers hold the truth, and how they are linked to our lives and our fate. Jagdish hung on to every word; his logical mind in a trance, in mathematical heaven. Whilst the rest of the guests slept, Jagdish and Gauba talked all night. Jagdish listened intently and asked many questions. Finally, it was morning. Time for Gauba to get dressed and report to work. Jagdish asked him to take the day off and let the conversation continue.

After breakfast, they continued to chat, oblivious of the rest of the residents of the house who had abandoned these possessed souls to their own devices. Leaving the two at home, the rest decided to step out and enjoy the cool breeze by the river, browse around and indulge in the street food, especially the puri aloo halwa the holy city of Haridwar is famous for. By evening, Jagdish's mind had stopped racing, his heart was calm and at peace. He thanked Gauba profusely for having taught him the fundamentals of something so precious that it was bound to alter his life forever. He was charged, inspired and filled with the bright light of enlightenment.

Thereafter, he went on to devour every book ever written on the subject. Every spare minute was spent on studying the subject and using it for calculations on self, family and friends. Jagdish's mind was ignited by this newfound knowledge, which he also wanted to try on strangers, whose life was a blank to him. He was searching for the right opportunity and it manifested itself in a unique manner. The family was on its way to its annual pilgrimage to Vaishno Devi, travelling in a three-tier compartment of the Jammu Tawi Express. This train is the first choice of the armed forces since it takes off from Jammu and chugs a long way to the Indian hinterland. It is also the favourite of pilgrims on their way to Katra from where they go on to start their climb to the Bhavan.

On the train, Jagdish chatted up the man sitting next to him. His name was Shyam Lal and Jagdish quickly calculated his 'name number', after asking him for his date of birth in order to calculate his destiny and psychic numbers. He offered the man a free consultation in numerology. He quickly combined his destiny, name and psychic numbers and was able to not just create a mental picture of his life in the past but also delve into the future. Jagdish was right about it all. Now, the person sitting across him also wanted a free reading. Before you knew it, the entire compartment was crowding around Guru 'Jagdish baba's' berth, eager for a consultation and a peek into their future. All the refreshments the Chaudhrys ordered were complimentary from then onwards.

People just wanted 'Guruji' to do was spell out their numbers. "Each of us have sadness, strife and struggles tucked away in the deep recesses of our heart. They all come pouring out as if a dam has burst when they are standing before a numerologist, a palmist or an astrologer. Hence it is important for people like us to hand out predictions with utmost sincerity and not comment on something unless we are sure it is accurate." Fame and acclaim slowly became his when many of his numerological predictions came true.

An author of two books on the subject: *Advanced Numerology* and *Prractical Numerology*, Jagdish relies a lot on numbers to show him the path and believes that if not a 100% accurate, numbers can help you sort at least 70% of your problems. While his first book helps people understand the power vested in numbers by the universe, the second one uses the Chaldean numerology system to help uncover the blueprint of a person's life using the number corresponding to their date of birth, birth certificate name and the name they are currently using.

He says in the preface of *Prractical Numerology*, "There is a mystical, divine relationship between numbers and the projection of life and all life events. Numbers are the letters of this language. In fact, every number has a unique vibration that has an influence upon the story of our life. Each one is a magical, mystical building block, defining divine logic in an understandable way. Together their relationships embody our collective, cumulative universe, and separately each number embodies our individual universe—our life path, our soul purpose and our larger destiny". He goes on to add, "To be forewarned is to be forearmed, and numerology reveals the blueprint of every human being's life."

However, being the humble human that he is he also adds a note of caution in *Advanced Numerology*, "Numerology is a study of numbers. It is not a perfect science since it gives about 65–70% information about any person...It is simply not possible for a numerologist to be 100% right. For that reason, a numerologist must always be careful and avoid harming those who come to him in good faith...I believe that a numerologist's asset is a true and indiscriminating love for the client, the seeker of truth." For him, the real utility of numerology is to motivate, elevate and inspire the seeker, to help him grapple with the rough tides of life.

Numerous tributes and testimonials can be found on his website www.jcchaudhry.com. These come from people whose lives changed dramatically after consultations with Jagdish. Sidhant Sahebji, Chairman of a media firm shares his experience of how his company was facing very sluggish growth. "J.C. Chaudhryji told us that the numbers of the Directors in our company did not match with the name of company. Earlier the name of our company was BKT Academy & Films Pvt. Ltd. and after Sir's suggestion we changed it to BKT Media Pvt. Ltd. and everything changed. Our speed changed and by the grace of God, despite the period of Covid-19 we are very successful. We are busy hosting shows, shooting films, etc. every day."

Jagdish applies numerology to solve a host of issues including auditing a company's compatibility with its people, calculating the right time for investment, naming newborns, assisting people in changing the spelling of their names as per numerology, calculating business partner compatibility and finding solutions for marital discord through numbers. However, what he does most is the compatibility audit of companies. According to him, a company can never do well if the top management does not match in numbers with the staff. Trusting his judgment on this front, both his sons never employ anyone without having their father do a numerological due diligence on the candidate.

Interestingly, Jagdish is able to find flaws through numbers in more ways than one. Once, he did not hire a young girl because he found the presence of discord in her house. On questioning she admitted that she had major differences with her mother-in-law. He had spotted this discord from the fact that her date of birth did not match with her house number!

According to Jagdish, a numerologist needs three numbers to know the inner nature and vibrations of a person, namely the psychic number that is related to the date of birth of a person; destiny number that is obtained by adding the date, month and year of birth; and the name number that is simply the numerological sum value of each letter of a person's name. He places the destiny number above the name number and the psychic number since this is directly linked to a person's karma, both in the present and past lives. The psychic number reveals the way a person looks at himself/herself. The name number has a strong influence on an individual's life, also impacting the psychic number though it is unable to affect the destiny number that is a congregation of a person's collective karma.

He has used numerology on himself too. This is how he found out that his date of birth was "totally wrong." How he stumbled on the right date, given the sorry state of documentation in those times is a story worth telling. Jagdish had believed his date of birth to be 1 August, 1949. However, as a numerologist, when he got down to matching his temperament and his life's trajectory thus far to his date of birth he was convinced that this date was wrong. None of his characteristics matched the date of birth listed in his records.

He first broached the subject with his father, Lalaji, who feigned total ignorance on the matter. His contention was that when it was tough to even put two square meals on the table, who cared about social niceties like birthdays! Besides, in those days record keeping was not even a norm. Jagdish then approached his primary school and met the Principal who told him that as per the records the date of birth was 1 August, 1949. However, they no longer had records dating back to the fifties and he was asked to go to the Police Station at Hodal.

A bewildered Jagdish calculated what his date of birth should be. On one side, he plotted his character and the events of his life and on the other, a list of plausible date of births that would actually match them. He concluded that as per his calculation it had to be sometime in November 1950. It was had to be a number divisible by 9 and could be 9, 18 or 27 November.

Now came the investigation. Jagdish went to the police station at Hodal. It was the norm for the village 'chowkidar' to register the list of births and deaths in the village at the police station. The officer in-charge informed him that they only had records for five years, after which they were transferred to the Chief Medical Officer's office in Gurgaon. At this office, Jagdish was told that all records for Sevli were lying in a basement next to Neelam Cinema in Faridabad, which was the CMO's office there.

Jagdish promptly knocked on this door. A clerk called Hanuman Prasad greeted him and a dusty file was pulled out from among the debris of dilapidated records. The year 1950 was unfortunately recorded in Urdu. Not one to give up, Jagdish quickly found someone at the local court who could translate it for him. He scrolled through the records: a boy was born to Nanak Chand, a resident of Sevli on 18 November, 1950! There was no other birth recorded on this date. Still curious, Jagdish asked him to check the record of 1 August, 1949. There was no record of a birth on that date. In fact, there was no mention of any child being born in the Chaudhry family that entire year. Jagdish immediately asked the CMO to give him an affidavit on a Rs. 2 Postal Order.

He realised that he would now gain an extra year and four months of service, which could give him a chance to retire as Deputy Director. The go getter got to work, writing to Punjab University that his records be set right in light of the new findings. He would go on to request the school administration to change his official records and add a year and half to his service. The University however refused asking why he had woken up thirty five years later to this reality. "I was disappointed at first; however, I accepted the fact. Atleast this new finding ensured I knew when to celebrate my actual birthday. Above all, I was glad that my numbers now corroborated with my fate."

The Chaudhry clan's new generation has achieved more in life through a numerological reorientation of their names. Jagdish's younger son who was named Manish at birth was rechristened Aakash, as the name did not vibrate with his date of birth and the records in school were changed. Aashish's name acquired a double A, which was a perfect match to his numbers. Jagdish also respelt the name of his brother's children who are now highly successful. His nephew Prashaant is an eye surgeon and his nieces are practising doctors in the UK and the US. Jagdish's contention is that certain numbers keep reappearing in your life. For some, number three and those divisible by it work. For others, it is 4, including the often misunderstood number 13, which works for Jagdish.

~

Jagdish's tryst with spirituality goes into the realms of meditation, chakra healing, gemology and astrology. Meditation as a practice consumed him for a very long time, till his wife surreptitiously drew him out of it. The innings with meditation is yet another compelling tale about his eager mind's constant quest to learn and perfect many new realms of knowledge.

His tryst with meditation is deeply connected to one of his students, Manish Barodia, son of a senior Director in Doordarshan.

Manish often complimented Chaudhry Sir for making even the dullest subjects engaging. One day, he invited Chaudhry Sir home, insisting that his father wanted to meet him and thank him for helping to shape Manish's life. Jagdish was touched when the father informed him that Manish felt Chaudhry Sir had the rare calibre to even "teach Biology to a donkey and make it respond positively". A bright spark, Manish was more inclined towards the arts and after completing a course in fine arts, went to the UK to pursue a career in advertising.

He kept in touch with Jagdish who was happy to hear his student was doing well. Many years later, he arrived at Jagdish's doorstep, dressed like a saint, radiating a sense of calm. He had arrived with a mission: to teach meditation to his Sir. The practical Jagdish wanted to know how meditation would help him. Manish said that with meditation Jagdish could gain three important things: close his eyes and let his mind wander anywhere; experience silence, a feeling of Zen, like a hundred zeroes filling his head; and with practice, learn how to make things happen with his mind power.

Jagdish started classes with his student who had turned into a spiritual Guru. The role reversal was extremely fulfilling. Every morning, Jagdish and Manish would gather in an empty room and practice mind control, or meditation. Like other realms, this one was mastered quickly too. And Jagdish began to take off with his mind on 'cruise control'. The first mind trick he did was to count the number of coins in Manish's pocket. When proved right, his Guru told him he was now in total control of his mind.

Jagdish remembers one of the many experiences where he used his mind control skills.

"I got a call from Mr. A.B. Singh handling the Bhuvaneshwar and Nagpur centres. He was in a state of panic, reporting a scuffle between students within the centre's premises. He himself was based in Bhuvaneshwar and was in touch with the manager at Nagpur who was reporting the chaos. I closed my eyes and went into a trance. In a few minutes, I saw a building made of red bricks. Inside it, all was quiet and there were no signs of chaos! I asked the manager if the building was made of red bricks. He confirmed. I told him to call the centre and check if everything had calmed down. He called back to confirm that it had."

Many such incidents strengthened his belief that through meditation he could take his mind wherever he wanted it to go. However, his preoccupation with meditation became so pronounced that his wife felt he was slowly turning into a saint, drifting away from worldly concerns. The protector in her came alive and one morning when Manish knocked on their door for his regular classes he was turned away, even as Jagdish awaited his arrival upstairs. The family met Jagdish upstairs and told him it was distracting him from his real goals in life and that karma was true meditation. From then on, it was goodbye to meditation though he and Manish kept in touch!

Meditation removed all traces of residual anger that Jagdish carried within him. It gave him the power to not just forgive and forget but also bless everyone, including competitors. Or as he puts it, he became a pro in the 'blessings' department. In this department one must also give Kamla full marks for stopping her husband from being obsessed with meditation. A very grounded woman, she has always anchored Jagdish. She passes off Jagdish's flights of fancy as strokes of genius, or the escapades of an experimental mind. But she always knows when it is time for her to put a stop to them, bringing her achiever husband back on track.

She reasons, "His mind is like a sponge, ready to absorb anything that catches his fancy. Such minds can easily get totally engrossed in something that consumes their complete life." And the job of a power woman like Kamla has been to be the voice of reason when her husband needed her to be. Her role extends to her sons as well. "Both Aashish and Aakash have used me as a conduit, a messenger to their father," she says. "I diffuse tensions and act as a lawyer who fights the case for both sides." Taking her husband's side is a must she also softens the blows when he clamps down too hard on their sons.

Spirituality, though a personal journey for Jagdish, also took the route of worship and prayer over the years. Religion has played a big role in his life and his utter devotion to Maa Vaishno Devi and the way the Goddess had blessed him in more ways than one, inspired him to thank her by building a shrine, a bit of heaven where devotees like him, otherwise caught up in the trials and tribulations of life could sit, pray, introspect and above all pay thanks for her divine blessings "I believe the Goddess gave me more than I ever desired or needed. I often refer to the phrase—kahan raja bhoj aur kahan gangu teli? (how can you compare a king to a fisherman?). She never held back her giving hand, endowing us with health, wealth and happiness and I often felt that we had not thanked her enough. So, the moment our profits exceeded our personal needs, I felt a strong urge to thank her in a way that she deserved," says Jagdish.

Jagdish wanted to build a Dham, a shrine where the Goddess would reside in all her glory, pomp and pageantry. A place that would replicate the experience of going to the Vaishno Devi shrine situated high up in the mountains. At the same time, it would be like a spiritual residency for city people in search of peace and a quiet moment with God. The first thing he needed was a site, a two-acre patch of land in a holy city. Jagdish travelled to Haridwar, Rishikesh, in and around his own village in Haryana but found nothing. Eventually, he was advised to try Vrindavan, the birthplace of Lord Krishna. He drove to Mathura with his architect. He found out that most large parcels of land were with a land shark called Narayan Das Aggarwal. They met him and asked for two acres of land to build a Dham. They were informed that he only had one piece of land, which was eighteen acres and had to be bought as a whole.

Jagdish went to see the plot. It was a flat and beautiful piece of land, almost like a grassy meadow where one could visualise Krishna the Shepherd God sitting under a tree as his cows grazed in the glassy glades. Jagdish stood transfixed. He recalls feeling a magnetic energy pulling him there. He knew that he had to invest in eight acres of land that he did not need and that it was here that his shrine, Maa Vaishno Devi Dham, had to be constructed. At that very moment, Jagdish handed over a token advance to Mr. Aggarwal and in 2002, the Chaudhrys bought the entire chunk of land under Jay Kay Trust, their not-for-profit Foundation.

Looking back, Jagdish is glad that he bought so much land. His trusted architect, Arun Verma, drew up a majestic plan. Ambitious and elaborate, it would be spread over twelve acres and the plan was so perfect that it left the entire family breathless with excitement. At the heart of it was a stunning statue of Maa Vaishno Devi 141 feet high. To witness its beauty one had to walk up a flight of meandering steps, flanked by majestic water bodies, beautiful gardens, caves and statues of Maa Vaishno Devi in her many avatars. The entire plan replicated the actual experience of walking to the original shrine, passing through tunnels and caves to see the beauty of the Goddess.

The blueprint was instantly approved and work began. What was proposed to take two years took seven, and the shrine was ready in 2010. A series of ceremonies marked the inauguration, some intimate and only involving the trustees and some having an attendance of over 6,000 devotees. Jagdish invited Dr. Karan Singh, a globally respected scholar, the erstwhile Maharaja of Jammu & Kashmir and also the Managing Trustee of the shrine in Katra to inaugurate the Dham. Besides the pristine temple, the sprawling gardens and the magnificent statue that won his Jay Kay Trust a name in the *Limca Book of Records*, there was also a full-fledged guest house for spiritual residency, a prayer house that can accommodate over 3,000 people, a few acres allotted to an organic farm and another acre for the cow shelter or gaushala.

Many a miracle was experienced while the temple was in the making. For one, the water around the shrine was hard water, not of drinkable quality. The architect suggested they dig a bore well that would cater solely to the shrine. He was not sure whether that water would be hard as well. Jagdish told the labourers to fold their hands and pray to the Goddess. Over a hundred people fervently prayed and lo and behold, the water that gushed from the earth was like manna from heaven, pure and clear.

There was an ancient mango tree with deep roots on the plot of land, an obstruction to the construction. Many attempts were made to uproot it, and plant it again in a different place. But nothing worked and Jagdish had a change of heart. He wanted to keep the tree. He was awed by its beauty and its sweet fruits. Soon after he decided the tree was to live, he dreamt that of it. In his dream, the tree and asked him why he wanted to kill it and deny the devotees of its magical fruits.

The tree whispered in his ears that if any woman were to devour its fruits she would be blessed with a child. Curious as always, Jagdish decided to try the magic on his own daughter-in-law. He plucked a few mangoes and requested her to eat them. Sure enough Meinal and Aakash were blessed with their eldest child. Miracle or coincidence, Jagdish was convinced that the tree had mystical powers and thanked the Goddess for its presence in the compound.

For Jagdish, the best part was, "The Dham would enable all those devotees who are unable to make the treacherous climb to the Bhawan in Katra receive Maa's blessings right here in Vrindavan. We aspired to bring Maa's divine Darshan closer to her devotees. Vrindavan, being a place of spiritual interest and inextricably linked to Lord Krishna, proved to be the perfect setting."

Both Kamla and Jagdish have anchored their lives on the two spiritual icons who are their Gods and guides. Their lives have revolved around the whimsical God, Lord Krishna, and the symbol of 'shakti', Maa Durga. They start their day in the prayer room at their home daily. The perfectly scultped images of these Gods are placed in this room. Kamla calls them her friends. "I share my worries with Maa Vaishno Devi who has been by my side ever since I went to her home in Jammu as a young bride. And Bal Gopal is my best friend. I talk my heart out to him."

Over twenty five lakh devotees throng the Dham each year from all over India for the Goddess's Darshan. Jagdish is now all set to add the Chaar Dhaam to the shrine, calling it, "my life's last big contribution to the world." At peace with himself and enjoying spending time with his grandchildren, he has handed over the reins of his empire to his capable sons. He is now busy delving into healing sciences like Lo Shu Grid and Chakra to enrich his store of knowledge. He writes books on these subjects, plays the role of Chairman Emeritus, and guide, philosopher and friend to the many aspiring youth who join Aakash Institute each year. He enjoys creating forums that will touch the life of children in rural India. His dream is to lead by example and motivate them to believe in his own life's guiding mantra: poverty is no bar to success. He constantly addresses the youth through inspirational talks where he shares experiences from his own life and the ups and downs that marked them. The motto 'no guts no glory' exemplifies this remarkable teacher, role model and self-made entrepreneur. For him, the biggest high is a victorious student's smile, the moment they find out that their hard work has paid off.

13

The Way Forward

Every one of us has a set of memories of precious moments spent with our parents like the time they lovingly dropped us off at the first day of school or stood outside the hall as we gave that one exam we dreaded the most. We cherish these memories and when we enter adulthood and as our parents grow older, they become even dearer to us. Before we know it, we take on the role of protective guardians to our parents and take care of them as if they have now turned into vulnerable children.

Aakash felt that sense of being the protective parent when he boarded a charter plane with his father in May 2021 to meet the dynamic partner with whom they had just signed a historic deal. This person who, in mettle and charisma, stood tall like his father, could be trusted to respect, nurture and take forward AESL just as the father-son duo had. Aakash felt a mix of powerful emotions during this momentous journey and he sensed his father's anxiety as they were travelling. Memories of forty long years of toil and sacrifices seemed to be rushing across his father's mindscape like one of the movies his father had watched many times. Except this time, Aakash was the one viewing the rushes of his father's mind in full cinemascope and experiencing what his father must feel about handing over the management of Aakash Educational Services Limited to someone else.

The father-son duo was heading to their first in person meeting with Byju Ravindran, the Ed-Tech genius with whom they had recently signed detailed papers, formally allowing the acquisition of AESL by his company, Byju's, at a whopping one billion rupees. This sign off made instant headlines and was perceived by the industry as a meeting of two titanic enterprises.

On the one hand, there was AESL, numero uno in the test-prep market, a brand built brick by brick by years of hard work, strife and admirable perseverance by a teacher of Biology and later fast-tracked into a corporate entity by Aakash, his son. And on the other, there was Byju's, a global market disrupter in the tech business, literally built overnight by a teacher who is also the son of schoolteachers. Both brands are equally accomplished and miles ahead of the competition in every way.

The trip to Bengaluru had come about because of Jagdish's request that he wanted to meet the man who would go on to own his Aakash at least once face to face. Since the entire process of signing the deal had been conducted over a series of online meetings on Zoom, while the two waves of the pandemic ravaged India, they had not met in person.

Byju was very apologetic that Chairman Sir had to make this trip, since he could not travel because he was looking after his father who had recently recovered from cancer and was totally homebound. Byju swore that had it not been for his father, he would have personally met Sir at his home in Delhi. Instead, Byju arranged a chartered flight to whisk the Chaudhrys to his home in Bengaluru. The meeting was a great success and Aakash instantly knew that his father, who could intuitively read a person, liked their young partner. In the course of the four hours they chatted and shared their views, he saw every crease of concern on his father's face vanish. Jagdish was happy and knew that Byju's was the perfect fit for his enterprise and the two would merge seamlessly.

Why did a profit-making, established business like Aakash think of liquidating its shares? Why did it seek out investors especially when AESL was acing all spheres of growth such as profitability, multiplication of centres, adoption of technology, online footprints, student enrollment, good results and the positioning as number one (AIPMT) in the fast-growing test-prep market of India? The answer is simple. Eliciting investment, they believe, is a sure shot path to growth for SMEs. A perfect way to circumvent the vicious cycle of reinvesting one's own capital. Besides, with dynamic partnerships come fresh energy and an instant adrenaline rush to do even better and reinvent the wheel.

The sign off with Byju's was the culmination of a long journey that began in 2013 and coincided with the many course correction steps the Chaudhrys took towards corporatising the business. It also coincided with Aakash taking over the driver's seat, while constantly looking up to his father for guidance and support. For him, bringing in partners was a step that had to be taken. He first proposed the idea of bringing in investors to the management at the start of 2013. Many coaching companies were already entering into partnerships and finding investors. There was a bit of resistance to begin with, but it took little convincing to get Chairman Sir on his side. Like always, Jagdish saw the merit in his son's proposal and like a perfect partner, agreed to walk that mile with him. Aakash is very proud of his father. He is yet to meet a man of his father's generation who remains so progressive and open to change.

In 2013 itself two large private equity funds, Actis Private Equity (a leading investor in growth markets across Africa, Asia and Latin America) and Apax Partners (a UK-based private equity fund known to help businesses and recognise innovative thinking), reached out to invest in AESL. Aakash spoke to his father who said that he was open to liquidate his holding. They were valued by the two funds at Rs. 1,100 crore. However, the business was still in its nascent stage then and the evaluators rightfully perceived it as too much of a family-run enterprise.

The deal did not work out, but their report clearly showed the Chaudhrys the points they had to address to turn themselves into a corporate entity, a national organisation run by a team of professionals. The Chaudhrys got down to business instantly, taking all the suggested steps. These included team building, talent scouting, creating SOPs for all the centres, experimenting with new technology and creating a corporate team. All of this was undertaken meticulously and steadfastly. By 2016, everything was in place, every gap filled, every weak link strengthened.

That year, Actis came back and gave them a healthy evaluation of Rs. 1,800 crore, but backed out once again after suggesting some important changes. The Chaudhrys decided to implement these suggestions rather than going partner hunting. However, the mountain came to Moses soon. At the end of the same year, three other funds—Kedaara Capital (an operationally oriented private equity firm pursuing control and minority investment opportunities in India), TA Associates (one of the early modern-era private equity firms in the United States which leads buyouts and minority recapitalisations) and TPG Capital (a.k.a Texas Pacific Group, an American private equity firm focused on leveraged buyouts and growth capital) sat down at the negotiation table with them.

This time, they were given a backhanded compliment while being valued at Rs. 2,200 crore, contending that their market had fully matured and they had reached the peak with no room for growth! On this point, the firms stepped back from the deal, while the Chaudhrys started researching market potential and realised instantly that the firms were way off the mark in calling the test-prep market a spent force.

Aakash pored over existing reports, research findings and articles to conclude that the test-prep market as a whole was worth over Rs. 50,000 crore. Whilst the segment AESL works in, namely preparing candidates for exams in engineering, medicine, and also steering a foundation programme, only controlled about Rs. 30,000 crore of the market. Hence an intelligent investor could grow in their existing segments as well as proliferate into the prep markets of MBA, UPSC, and banks, etc. These competitive exams also have a very large captive audience.

Every time an investor came along, AESL's evaluation shot up. For instance, Carla Hill (another large PE firm), evaluated them at Rs. 3,500 crore just two years later. Though this deal too fell through, the generous evaluation gave AESL the confidence to get themselves listed and consider going public. They got the papers ready, the red herring prospectus prepared and embarked on a very ambitious road show wherein Aakash and his team met 108 investors across the globe in a span of forty five days. The response was overwhelming to put it mildly.

Aakash recalls coming back feeling elated, confident and buoyant, only to have the deadly missile of the IL&FS fiasco bust his dream. Overnight, the market turned murky, its edifice shaken, and AESL's bankers asked them to hold on. Aakash followed this advice, dipping into the deep reservoir of patience his father had instilled in him. In this sense, he truly respects the old school business leaders who take the ups with as much grace as the downs. Aakash often wonders how an impatient millennial would have reacted in the same situation.

Patience paid off and in March 2019, Blackstone reached out to them, evaluating AESL at Rs. 3,600 crore. They saw great value in the business. This time the deal went through and Jagdish was able to liquidate 37% of his shares at Rs. 1,350 crore as they valued the chain at USD 500 million (over Rs. 3,545 crore). With Jagdish having accepted the role of Chairman Emeritus, Aakash took on the entire responsibility of managing the day-to-day functioning of AESL.

AESL was keen to give more teeth to the fast-emerging market of K-12, which also is the feeder market for the medical and engineering test-prep courses. AESL was studying the market and exploring the way forward. A company called Meritnation had caught Aakash's attention. Its content-led Ed-Tech offering for the K-12 market was unique. Aakash had once met the founder Pawan Chauhan and been extremely impressed by his vision.

Industries can only flourish through exchange of ideas and a free-flowing relationship between competitors. Hence, as a practice, Aakash used to meet with all the competition. This was how he met Pawan for the first time. Aakash had liked his honest approach and invigorating energy and had quietly studied the strides Pawan had made by creating a content-led online learning platform for school students. He was impressed by how Pawan attached the company to Infoedge and used their 'edge' over technology to his advantage. Founded by Pawan, an IIM Graduate and his partner Ritesh Hemrajani in 2009, Meritnation's forum of live classes interested AESL very much.

Aakash met Pawan, did his due diligence and decided to own the company wholly, closing the deal at Rs. 100 crore. The idea was not to absorb it into AESL's operations but to let it grow on its own steam. Hence it was positioned as a division of AESL, allowing it to work as an independent entity, while acting as a great feeder market to AESL's business. Thankfully, the decision paid off and this partnership has strengthened remarkably well over the years.

Pawan was the one Byju Ravindran reached out to first in June 2020. Byju knew Pawan and was eager to acquire Meritnation. He was also extremely upbeat about Aakash, and keen to strengthen his footprints in the test-prep market. He enquired about AESL from Pawan and was reassured by him that not only would AESL be a progressive partner to Meritnation, it also understood the test-prep market better than any other player. Besides, like most people, Pawan too was in total awe of Chairman Sir and the empire he had built.

With this reassurance, Byju reached out to AESL just when the first wave of the pandemic had hit India hard and the nation was grappling with an unprecedented lockdown. Like any sharp businessman, Byju felt that given that this was a pandemic year and AESL a brick-and-mortar brand, it would be experiencing a drop in business as its centres would be shut. He felt he would end up buying it at a good price. He was surprised when AESL shared its numbers, which showed that 2020 had actually been a growth year! AESL had skillfully transitioned into online classes, ensuring that all their students across the spectrum were well prepared for their entrance exams. The numbers for the year kindled Byju's interest even further and he offered a total buy out at Rs. 4,300 crore, an amount at which Aakash refused to sign point blank. The negotiation went on to 5,300 crore and then 6,000, finally closing at 6,800 crore in October, part monetised and part equity.

Aakash was happy with the final offer and took the deal to his father who gave him the nod. Aakash had promised to try and close the deal at Rs. 8,000 crore at the least. However, given that it was a

A loving grandmother and a mother-in-law today, Kamla Chaudhry says that her favourite parenting mantra has always been to practise patience and be a true friend to both her children. (Roy Henderson)

Aashish Chaudhry hopes that his daughters Aashvika and Anyesha will take an interest in the healthcare business when they grow up. (Roy Henderson)

J.C. Chaudhry is determined to instil enough confidence in his grandchildren so that they have the emotional wherewithal to grow into whoever they aspire to be. (Roy Henderson)

Kamla Chaudhry is friend, comrade-in-arms and confidante to her granddaughter. She satisfies her every whim. (Roy Henderson)

Aashish Chaudhry has big dreams for his daughter. But he does not want to influence her in any way when she chooses her career path. The decision should and will be entirely her individual choice. (Roy Henderson)

Aakash Chaudhry makes an effort to spend time with his daughter, who he feels will soon fly away, study overseas and see the world. (Roy Henderson)

J.C. Chaudhry addressing a gathering at the inauguration of the Chaar Dham. ©J.C. Chaudhry

The Chaar Dham (Mahadev Dham, Radhe Krishan Dham, Shani Dham and Maa Vaishno Devi Dham) was inaugurated on 23 August 2021. ©J.C. Chaudhry

Spirituality is the cornerstone of J.C. Chaudhry's (seen here with three of his close friends) life. He is thankful for the grace of God and the unwavering support of his friends. ©J.C. Chaudhry

Left: J.C. Chaudhry celebrating International Numerology Day on 18 November with Rajendra Pratap Gupta (left), Chairman, Internet Governance Forum of the UN. ©J.C. Chaudhry

Right: The Guinness Book of Records awarded J.C. Chaudhry the Guinness World Record for the most viewers of a Numerology lesson live-streamed on YouTube, calling it a pioneering achievement of 2022. ©J.C. Chaudhry

Cherished moments from a leisure trip to Pahalgam, Jammu and Kashmir, with wife Kamla. ©J.C. Chaudhry

The motto 'no guts no glory' exemplifies J.C. Chaudhry, a remarkable teacher, role model and one of India's most successful entrepreneurs.(Roy Henderson)

pandemic year, Jagdish was sensitive to the situation and felt that it was a good amount at which to let go of his 'baby'. Besides, he felt reassured by the fact that the company that was buying them out belonged to the industry and hence, would be as interested in taking the brand forward as them. This was the real clincher. Byju Ravindran had achieved so much in so little time. Also, he was genuinely interested in expanding into the test-prep market and saw merit in the classroom format which Aakash was a master of.

They made contact in December over a Zoom call by which time Aakash had convinced Blackstone about the sale as well. The term sheet was handed over to the Chaudhrys with an expression of interest in the first week of January 2021. It took their lawyers three months to put all the documents together and on 3 April, 2021, the deal was signed. Both Byju and the Chaudhrys were clear that the day they signed the deal had to be equally lucky for both partners and hence 3 May was chosen. It was a very emotional day for Jagdish and in a voice filled with feeling, he told Byju that what he was handing over to him was a product of his blood, sweat and tears. Byju assured him that he would guard it with his life. His words resonated well with Jagdish and dispelled his fears.

Byju has stood by his word and has already started to move his own test-prep business into Aakash. Their teams are buzzing with ideas about how they can grow, and what they can add. The adrenaline is flowing and Aakash is once again ready to soar to the skies.

~

So, shall we call it Aakash 2? A new phase for the company and for the family that gave it life? The Chaudhrys were happy that with Byju in the driver's seat, Aakash would grow and proliferate further, keeping the flag flying high. As for Jagdish, he is all set to get fully involved with what he calls his two swan songs: the creation of the four Dhams in his ashram so people in search of God who are unable to trek to Katra can find the divine in Vrindavan itself. And then there is the epic movie he has always dreamt of producing on Maa Vaishno Devi. He has invited none other than the great Ramanand Sagar's son to direct this dream project. Apart from these pursuits, he sees numerology fast replacing the demands of his teaching life.

Aakash promises to stay emotionally involved with AESL and has assured his teams that he will be with them till the final merger happens in June 2022 and the 30% equity is formally transferred to the Chaudhrys. AESL thereafter will be a division of Byju's and whether Aakash continues in his role as CEO will be a decision for them to take. Regardless of that decision, Aakash is keen to explore the realm of sustainability and create something that will empower the environment. He plans to work in the field of renewable energy, exploring solutions to the problem of plastic and environmental degradation in a commercial way.

His dream is to take a year off to find his own path. He entered the family business two decades ago and ever since, worked round the clock to nurture his father's dream and do complete justice to it. Now, he longs to spend time with his children, who he feels will soon fly away, study overseas, and see the world. He wants to instill enough confidence in them so that they have the emotional wherewithal to grow into whoever they want to be.

Aakash is confident that the enterprise his father created will flourish and reach greater heights with Byju at the helm. In his opinion, Byju is the ideal man to step into the inimitable J.C. Chaudhry's shoes.

14

Creating A Legacy From A Dream

Whoever coined the phrase 'it is all in the numbers' possibly had this genius teacher in mind. Someone in whose life numbers have held the highest place of reverence. For Jagdish Chandra Chaudhry, they are as precious as the Bible, the Bhagavad Gita or the Koran. Right from calculating his own date of birth against a Himalayan pile of misleading records to subliminally sizing up every person he included in his professional and personal life through Numerology, J.C. Chaudhry, the educationist, has placed this ancient science of numbers on the same pedestal as Botany or Maths.

The teacher in him dreamt of taking this science to the classroom level in order to give it the academic respect it deserves so that a class full of eager young minds could learn the science of Numerology and apply it to the realm of life, allowing humans to rely on numbers to take more 'calculated and careful decisions.' Jagdish hoped to make this dream his final project in life. It was the spiritual field he would allow his energy to be diverted to, once his worldly roles were done and dusted.

The doer, thinker, teacher and mystic has finally turned this dream into reality. Now that Aakash Educational Institute is touching the skies with his son Aakash and partner Byju Ravindran in the pilot's seat, J.C. Chaudhry is training his energy on a quest that has lasted 37 years and continues to be the axis around which most of his life spins—sharing the wondrous science of Numerology with the world, lending to it the depth, gravitas and legitimacy it deserves.

Not all legacies are made of brick and mortar. Some are made of dreams which turn into reality. "All my life, I asked myself what I could give back as my gift to my nation and the world. At the core, I am a teacher first and the passion to teach has thrived in me. Very often, my subconscious asked me was why we could not create an educational institution like the Indian Institute of Management (IIM) in the field of Numerology. If IIMs are for management education, why shouldn't we establish an Indian Institute of Numerology (IIN) that will be the ultimate Gurukul for Numerology? State-of-the art facilities, ancient and spiritual in its academic offerings, with science at its heart," says Jagdish.

Hence, IIN was born as a knowledge hub where people can learn and practice Numerology with the hope of helping future generations to enhance their lives. Jagdish plans to mould it into the first international-level institute that will produce the finest numerologists globally. A one-of-a-kind institute that will open its gates for people from all walks of life and corners of the world interested in the 'power of numbers'.

Every large leap calls first for some small steps to create the rhythm and pace. And thus, was born the second pillar of J.C. Chaudhry's legacy: the decision to establish a special day to celebrate the science of Numerology all over the world. IND or International Numerology Day was born on 18 November 2021. "Numerology is like the nectar that created a miraculous aura in my life. I felt this inner urge to share this nectar of knowledge with the world. I chose the date, 18 November, not because it was my birthday but because it was through Numerology that I had discovered my own date of birth. I am sure there are many in this world like me who are unaware of their real date of birth! I dedicate this day to them," says Jagdish.

The first International Numerology Day was attended by seekers from over 10 nations and presided over by Rajendra Pratap Gupta, Chairman of the newly formed Internet Governance Forum of the

United Nations. Seeing IND come alive gave the biggest seeker of this science, J.C. Chaudhry, as much mystical joy and happiness as he had experienced when he discovered through Numerology that 18 November is the actual day he was born.

A particular science could be ancient but its implementation and amplification must adopt modern tools of technology. Numerology, practised across ancient Egypt, Mesopotamia, China, India and Greece, traditionally grew in tiny pockets or isolated islands with accomplished numerologists never enjoying the privilege of communicating with each other effectively. This inspired Jagdish to think deeply. "People who lived 2000 or 3000 years ago battled with the barrier of time and space, but the Internet and digital technology have resolved this easily. I get queries from people around the world and can connect with numerologists living in the farthest corners of the universe through the Internet. My dream was to bring them all together on one platform and create a global network of numerologists. I brainstormed on what I could do and the idea evolved: create an International Numerology Forum (INF), headquartered in the United Arab Emirates (UAE), with members from every nation of the world."

Apart from educating people, the Forum's agenda is to create a thriving platform where bright minds can discuss and explore this science. He envisions INF also hosting an annual gathering of numerologists at its headquarter where the best ideas and practices for global development of the science would be shared.

Not one for slow progress, Jagdish now sought an accelerator, a single step that would make the world sit up and take notice. His head was teeming with ideas that would instantly bring INF, IIN and IND under the global eye. Like lightning it struck him, one morning, that he must handpick one of the five global gateways to glory: the United Nations, the Nobel Prize, the Olympics, the Oscars or the Guiness Book of World Records. A world record seemed the easiest route to take and, smiling broadly, he went about setting a world record by hosting what he hoped would be the most viewed Numerology session live-streamed on YouTube ever.

The original plan was to host a hybrid session that would be held online as well as in real time. His team was eager to do this but the Omicron wave ruined the chances of gathering a large number of people under one roof. So, on 1 January 2022, a Numerology lesson was live-streamed on YouTube on the 'Power of Name—Fourth Dimension of Life'. The session highlighted how people could calculate their 'name number', check if the name brings a positive aspect to their lives and calculate the scope of correction to make their name vibrate with their date of birth. The session was attended by nearly 6,000 viewers during the live-streaming, the highest participation for such a session worldwide. Not only did the Guinness Book of Records confer him with the Guinness World Record for the most viewers of a Numerology lesson live-streamed on YouTube, the Guinness World Record London office has set up a new category itself for this feat, calling it a pioneering achievement for the year 2022.

Now channeling all his energy, grit and determination on taking his three pillars forward, J.C. Chaudhry the globally acclaimed numerologist dedicates this momentous award to, "Pythagoras and all those unknown, unsung mathematicians and numerologists who took the science forward." A teacher at heart, his dream is to see the subject included in the middle-school curriculum one day. If it is all in the numbers, then the sooner we master them the better being his message to the world.